GAY AND LESBIAN WRITERS

Walt Whitman

GAY AND LESBIAN WRITERS

James Baldwin

Allen Ginsberg

Adrienne Rich

Sappho

Walt Whitman

Oscar Wilde

GAY AND LESBIAN WRITERS

Walt Whitman

Arnie Kantrowitz

Lesléa Newman
Series Editor

CHELSEA HOUSE
PUBLISHERS
A Haights Cross Communications Company ®

Philadelphia

CHELSEA HOUSE PUBLISHERS

VP, NEW PRODUCT DEVELOPMENT Sally Cheney
DIRECTOR OF PRODUCTION Kim Shinners
CREATIVE MANAGER Takeshi Takahashi
MANUFACTURING MANAGER Diann Grasse

Staff for WALT WHITMAN

EXECUTIVE EDITOR: Matt Uhler
EDITORIAL ASSISTANT: Sarah Sharpless
PHOTO EDITOR: Sarah Bloom
SERIES AND COVER DESIGNER: Takeshi Takahashi
LAYOUT: EJB Publishing Services

A Haights Cross Communications Company ®

http://www.chelseahouse.com

First Printing

9 8 7 6 5 4 3 2 1

Library of Congress Cataloging-in-Publication Data
Kantrowitz, Arnie, 1940-
  Walt Whitman / Arnie Kantrowitz.
    p. cm. — (Gay and lesbian writers)
  Includes index.
  ISBN 0-7910-8222-9 (alk. paper) — ISBN 0-7910-8387-X (pbk.) 1.
Whitman, Walt, 1819-1892. 2. Poets, American—19th century—Biography.
3. Gay men—United States—Biography. I. Title. II. Series.
  PS3232.K25 2005
  811'.3—dc22
                          2005001590

Cover: Library of Congress, LC-DIG-cwpbh-00752

All links and web addresses were checked and verified to be correct at
the time of publication. Because of the dynamic nature of the web,
some addresses and links may have changed since publication and may
no longer be valid.

For Larry Mass, my camerado.

Acknowledgments
Gay Wilson Allen, Martin Duberman,
Jonathan Ned Katz, Gene Stavis

TABLE OF CONTENTS

MANY YEARS AGO, IN 1970 to be exact, I began my career as a high school student. Those were the dark ages, before cell phones and CD players, before computers and cable TV, before the words "gay" and "pride" ever—at least to my knowledge— appeared in the same sentence. In fact, I remember the very first time I saw the word "gay" appear in a newspaper. It was in the early 1970s, a year after the 1969 Stonewall riots when a group of butches and drag queens fought back against a police raid on a gay bar, sparking what was then known as the "gay liberation movement." I was sitting in our Long Island living room with my brothers, my parents, and some visiting relatives. One of the adults picked up the newspaper, read a headline about the anniversary of Stonewall and said in a voice dripping with disapproval, "Well, all I can say is *gay* certainly meant something different in my time." There were a few murmurs of agreement, and then the matter was dropped. I learned very quickly that this subject was taboo in the Newman household.

Not that I had any inkling that I would grow up to be a lesbian. All I knew was that I didn't want to get married and have children, I wasn't interested in boys, and all I wanted to do was read books, write poetry, and spend time with my best friend, Vicki, who lived three houses away. My friendship with Vicki was strictly platonic, but even so, taunts of "Leslie the lezzie, Leslie the lezzie" followed me up and down the hallways of

Jericho High School. (I changed my name from Leslie to Lesléa when I was sixteen largely because, due to my gender-free name, I was, much to my horror, enrolled in the boys' gym class.)

Interestingly enough, Vicki was never once teased for being a lesbian; did my classmates know something I didn't know?

In 1973 I left home to attend the University of Vermont. There was no gay/straight alliance on campus, nor were there courses in gay literature or gay history. Though I studied the poetry of Gertrude Stein, I was never led to believe that Alice B. Toklas was anything more than the poet's housekeeper and cook. Though I studied Walt Whitman's work and read the novels of James Baldwin, there was never any mention of either man's sexuality. And even though I still was unaware of my own sexuality, I knew somehow that I was "different." I did not want the same things most of the young women around me wanted, namely a husband and children. I did not know being a lesbian was a possibility. Since I wasn't interested in boys "that way," I simply thought I was not a sexual being.

What saved me was the Beat movement, and specifically the Beat poets: Allen Ginsberg, Peter Orlovsky, Gary Snyder, Anne Waldman, and Ted Berrigan, all of whom became my teachers when I hitchhiked out to Boulder, Colorado, and enrolled in Naropa Institute's Jack Kerouac School of Disembodied Poetics. The Beats were unabashedly sexual. Allen and Peter were clearly a couple; there was also a pair of lesbians on the faculty who made no secret of the fact that they lived together. I learned about Sappho and the island of Lesbos; I learned that Virginia Woolf and Vita Sackville-West were not merely pen pals; I learned that Emily Dickinson had a correspondence with her sister-in-law Susan Huntington Dickinson that some interpreted as romantic. And though these women may or may not have been lesbians, the discovery that women could be primary in each other's lives in a passionate way filled me with a sense of excitement and hope. Finally I realized that I wasn't a freak. There were others like me. A world of possibilities opened up before my eyes.

In 1999, I was invited back to my alma mater to be inducted into the Jericho High School Hall of Fame. The world had changed in many ways since I graduated in 1973. The words "gay" and "lesbian" now appeared in many newspapers across the country on a regular basis, and the gay, lesbian, bisexual, and transgendered community even had its own newspapers and magazines. In 1977, Harvey Milk, the first openly out politician in this country, had been elected as a San Francisco City Supervisor (tragically he was assasinated in his office the following year). Most large cities had gay and lesbian pride parades during the month of June and many high schools had gay straight alliances (Concord High School in Concord, Massachusetts started the first GSA in 1989). The "gayby boom" had begun as more and more lesbians and gay men were starting families, and the gay marriage movement was going strong.

Since graduating from high school, my life had changed dramatically as well. In 1988 I met the woman of my dreams and a year later, on September 10, 1989, we celebrated our relationship with a lifetime commitment ceremony (On September 10, 2004, we renewed our vows before a justice of the peace, making our fifteen-year marriage legal in the state of Massachusetts). I had published close to thirty books, most of which had gay or lesbian content, including the picture book, *Heather Has Two Mommies*, which became one of the most controversial and challenged books of the 1990s. And I had become a political activist, speaking out for the rights of lesbians and gay men every chance I could.

When I was inducted into Jericho High School's Hall of Fame, I was invited to come to campus to give a speech at a school assembly. It was only upon arrival that I was informed that the students knew only one thing about me: I was an author. They did not know the titles of my books and they did not know I was a lesbian. Consequently, I had the unexpected opportunity to come out to an entire high school population. If the students were surprised, they did not show it. Jericho students are nothing if not polite. But they did ask interesting questions. They wanted to know if I had dated boys when I was in high school (yes); they wanted to know how old I was when I came out (twenty-seven); they wanted to know if I wished that I were straight (no, but sometimes I wish my hair was). At one point the questions came to a halt, so I decided to ask my audience, "What is it like for gay and lesbian students today at Jericho High School?" The auditorium was quiet for a moment and then a boy called out, "We don't have any gay students."

About a year later, I received an email from a Jericho High School alumna who graduated in June of 1999. She told me she was a lesbian and had known so since she was fifteen years old. She had been at my induction assembly, but did not feel comfortable coming out in front of her peers that day, or even privately to me. Only after she graduated from high school and went away to college did she feel safe enough to be out. Clearly many things had changed since I'd attended Jericho High School and many things had not.

A book is a powerful thing, and literature can change people's lives. If I had read a biography about a lesbian writer when I was in high school, I truly believe my life would have been vastly different. I might very well have been spared years of pain and confusion because I would have known that a life very much like the one I am now living is possible. If the books in this series had been on the Jericho High School curriculum in 1999, perhaps the young woman who sent me an email would have felt safe enough to come out of the closet before graduation.

It is my hope that this book and others like it will help high school students know that not everyone is heterosexual, and that gay, lesbian, bisexual, and transgendered people can and do live happy, productive, inspiring, and creative lives. The writers included in this series have certainly left their mark on society with their award-winning works of poetry and prose. May they inspire us all to be exactly who we are with pride and celebration.

—Lesléa Newman, 2004

WALT WHITMAN: SONG OF HIMSELF

Growing up on Long Island in the 1960s and 1970s, the name "Walt Whitman" was very familiar to me. I did not associate his name with poetry however; but rather with jeans (which we called dungarees back then) and earrings and pocketbooks, for I spent many a weekend at the Walt Whitman Mall in South Huntington, Long Island, shopping with my friends. I believe we did study Whitman's most famous poem, "Leaves of Grass" at some point in high school, but the first time I took an interest in his poetry was years later when I was studying poetics with Allen Ginsberg at Naropa Institute in Boulder, Colorado.

I was reading Allen's book, *Howl and Other Poems*, when I came upon "A Supermarket in California." In this poem, Allen Ginsberg imagines seeing Walt Whitman in a supermarket:

> "I saw you, Walt Whitman, childless, lonely old
> grubber, poking among the meats in the refrigerator
> and eyeing the grocery boys …"
>   (Howl and Other Poems, page 29)

And later the poem asks:

> "Where are we going, Walt Whitman? The doors

close in an hour. Which way does your beard point
tonight?"

(Howl and Other Poems, page 30)

As I read the above poem, it suddenly dawned on me: Walt
Whitman was gay. Just like Allen. Just like me. Why else would
he be eyeing the grocery boys? Why else would Allen Ginsberg
choose to immortalize him rather than any other poet in
"Supermarket in California"?

I decided to study up on Walt Whitman and I'm glad I did,
because truth be told, if I was stranded on a desert island and
could only take one book of poetry with me, that book would
be, without a doubt, "Leaves of Grass." The book celebrates,
uplifts, inspires, and encompasses all of life. Every time I read
it, I notice something new about it. There is no other work of
poetry quite like it in the entire world.

The very first line of "Leaves of Grass" strikes me as radical:

"I celebrate myself …"

Those three little words alone are enough to make me stop
and think. Raised in America and surrounded by mainstream
culture, I was not taught to celebrate myself. As a young girl
and woman, I was told that I was too short, too fat, and too
loud. My hair was too curly. I wasn't feminine enough. My feelings towards other women were something to be denied and
hidden, not celebrated. The thought of "celebrating" myself was
nothing short of revolutionary. I believe the notion of accepting
and loving oneself completely, and finding oneself worthy of
"celebration" can totally transform a person's life. Whitman's
proclamation "I celebrate myself" allows me to celebrate
myself, too.

Opening "Leaves of Grass" at random, I find other words,
phrases and lines that are no less extraordinary.

"I am of old and young, of the foolish as much as the wise,"

Having studied Buddhism, I recognize its influence on Whitman's writing immediately. Buddhists believe that all sentient beings, from the largest to the smallest, are connected. (The first time I attended a Buddhist meditation retreat held on the hottest day of the year in a stuffy hall that had no air-conditioning, I was told in no uncertain terms that it was forbidden to kill a mosquito or a fly). Whitman's words clearly underscore this belief. He is one with everyone:

"A learner with the simplest, a teacher of the thought fullest …"

"A farmer, mechanic, or artist … a gentleman, sailor, lover or quaker,
A prisoner, fancy-man, rowdy, lawyer, physician or priest."

Walt Whitman wrote in a way that no other poet had written before. Instead of sticking to standard forms, he wrote long, loose lines full of images and lists. His poetry is infused with his spirituality and his respect for and love of nature. One of my favorite passages of "Leaves of Grass" has to do with grass itself:

"A child said, What is the grass? fetching it to me with full hands;
How could I answer the child? … I do not know what it is any more than he …"

Whitman then proceeds to give us a list of gorgeous images to describe ordinary grass as if it were a miracle of creation (which it is!). The images include "the flag of my disposition," "the handkerchief of the Lord," and "the beautiful uncut hair of graves."

When Emily Dickinson was asked, "What is poetry?" she answered by saying, "If I feel physically as if the top of my head were taken off, I know that is poetry." Every time I read the line "the beautiful uncut hair of graves" I feel my own hair stand up at the back of my neck. Whitman's poetry passes Emily Dickinson's test with flying colors.

It makes me sad to think that Walt Whitman could not own his passionate feelings towards other men openly during his lifetime. As Arnie Kantrowitz tells us in his wonderful biography, the scholar John Addington Symonds asked Whitman, towards the end of his life, if he was open to having readers interpret his words in their own way (implying that some would interpret his lines as describing same-sex love). Whitman's answer clearly shows that he found the possibility of having anyone read same-sex passion into his work very upsetting. He then went on to assure Symonds of his own heterosexuality, telling him he has had six children. I can't help thinking of the Shakespeare line's line from Act III, Scene II of Hamlet: "The lady doth protest too much, methinks." There is no real evidence that Whitman had one child, let alone six. The fact that he had to invent a heterosexual marriage in order to protect his image as a poet must have been quite painful to him.

Luckily we now live in the 21st century and we can celebrate Walt Whitman as a poet and as a man whose greatest passions were for other men. We celebrate all of him, not part of him. And thus we celebrate ourselves.

—Lesléa Newman

one

Do I Contradict Myself?

Do I contradict myself?
Very well then I contradict myself,
(I am large, I contain multitudes.)

—"Song of Myself"

LIKE MANY OTHER MEN WHO loved men, John Addington Symonds saw in Walt Whitman's poetry the first published proclamation that same-sex love, rather than being sinful or criminal or sick, is a beautiful experience. Symonds, a married homosexual scholar from England, was one of Whitman's most ardent followers and had been writing to his idol for 20 years. Whitman had received impassioned letters and visits from other such men, among them Oscar Wilde, the urbane Irish playwright; Bram Stoker, the author of *Dracula;* Charles Warren Stoddard, an Englishman who had moved to the South Pacific islands to be free of society's restraints; and Edward Carpenter, an innovative English socialist writer. All had sought Whitman's personal guidance because they were inspired by his bold words:

> I will sing the song of companionship,
> I will show what alone must finally compact these [men],
> I believe these are to found their own ideal of manly
>   love, indicating it in me,
> I will therefore let flame from me the burning fires
>   that were threatening to consume me,
> I will lift what has too long kept down those
>   smouldering fires,
> I will give them complete abandonment,
> I will write the evangel-poem of comrades and of love.
> For who but I would understand love with all its
>   sorrow and joy?
> And who but I should be the poet of comrades?

But in 1890, when Whitman was 71 years old and in failing health, Symonds asked him a disturbing question that he didn't know how to answer:

In your conception of Comradeship, do you contemplate the possible intrusion of those semi-sexual emotions and actions which no doubt do occur between men? I do not ask, whether you approve of them, or regard them as a necessary part of the relation? But I should much like to know whether *you are prepared to leave them to the inclinations & the conscience of the individuals concerned?*

How could Whitman reply to such a letter? If he told the truth, it could undo all the years of effort he'd put into creating the public image of himself as the robust and masculine common man: the man who had sounded his "barbaric yawp" over the rooftops of the world. It might well destroy his dream of being remembered as America's national bard. But if he lied, it would betray the most honest and intimate lines of his homoerotic "Children of Adam" and "Calamus" poems. It would betray the men whom he had loved and who had loved him; and it would disappoint the male-loving men who had felt alone in a world that denied their very existence until they had read his words. Which did he want more: the immortality he might purchase with a lie, or the integrity that might cost him everything he had worked for? After much consternation, he decided to lie.

Symonds' question had been asked as delicately as possible. It did not actually inquire whether Whitman himself had had sex with other men. Nor did it even imply that Whitman necessarily advocated such sex. Symonds went on to say that since some men have "a strong natural bias toward their own sex," he understood the objections to the idea that the poems were "calculated to encourage ardent & *physical* intimacies." (If such intimacies were to occur, however, Symonds said he personally did not believe it would be "prejudicial to social interests.") His question merely suggested the *contemplation* of a "*possible intrusion*" of "*semi-sexual*" feelings and actions, without defining any of those terms explicitly. It was a proper Victorian question from a proper Victorian scholar, whose books attempted to explore the beauty of male–male sex by studying the culture of ancient Greece, where sex between men was idealized in elegant vase paintings and male teachers had reportedly had sexual relations with their male students—all safely removed in time and place from 19th-century Anglo-American culture.

The Victorian era was an age of sexual hypocrisy. Covering up was the fashion of the day. With the exception of some female shoulders bared only in ballrooms, people wore clothing that hid their bodies from their chins to the ground. To show off their wealth, middle-class citizens ostentatiously covered their carpets with rugs, their tables with floor-length cloths, and their windows with several layers of curtains. In refined conversation, graphic words like "arm" and "leg" were avoided in favor of more refined words like "limb." In the strictest homes, the "limbs" of the pianos were discreetly covered with lace pantalets, and the books of male and female authors were kept on separate shelves.

The "Gilded Age" that followed the Civil War in America kept not just same-sex relations but all of its sexuality in the closet. Although passion was not uncommon within marriage, it was generally not discussed. Victorian gentlemen took their pleasures with painted prostitutes in opulent brothels, decorated with crystal chandeliers and scarlet-flocked wallpaper and overstuffed couches, while their families waited at home in their genteel parlors and turned their eyes away from anything that might be construed as erotic. Civility and social customs were of high importance and anything suggestive of nature and its untamed urges was discouraged and even shunned. It was a time of national expansion and economic growth, a time of inveterate optimism, and until the 20th century, when "muck-rakers" began to reveal sordid corruption in business and politics, society wanted to think of itself as sunny and wholesome.

Polite people didn't admit to improper feelings: for all intents and purposes, anything that went unspoken simply didn't exist. Men had always had sex with other men. The raids of the English male brothels called "molly houses" in the early 18th century showed that those who preferred such sex were already considered to belong to a particular category or social type, but the American counterpart has yet to be found by historians. Until late in the century, when the medical term "homosexual" was introduced, there was no popular language with which to discuss these men. When ladies weren't present, words from earlier centuries like *buggery* or *sodomy* might refer to specific acts. Otherwise, even in the laws that forbade it, homosexuality was generically called "the crime against nature."

Whitman had boldly confronted such hypocrisy. His poetry celebrated the natural world that included the love between men (but even he didn't discuss the love between women, which was an even more invisible form of homosexuality). To readers of our more sexually expressive era his words might seem tame, but in poems like "Native Moments" he had written more openly than anyone in his time about sex:

> Give me the drench of my passions, give me life
>   coarse and rank,
> I am for those who believe in loose delights, I share
>   the midnight orgies of young men,
> I dance with the dancers and drink with the drinkers,
> The echoes ring with our indecent calls, I pick out
>   some low person for my dearest friend,
> He shall be lawless, rude, illiterate, he shall be one

condemn'd by others for deeds done,
I will play a part no longer, why should I exile
myself from my companions?

For most proper readers, this couldn't mean what it said. They decided that his poems must be about normal, lusty boys being pals together, enjoying the rough powers of youth. He had, after all, written of his admiration for sturdy working-class young men, the muscle that had produced America's growing economic success. But even that sort of crudeness was not acceptable in dignified homes, in many of which he was considered a foul-mouthed libertine.

Although Whitman wrote of other matters—politics and patriotism, nature and identity, death and spirituality—many decent people had shunned or actually burned his book. He had even been fired from a job for his writing. Yet he worked hard to rebuild his reputation, reworking his one volume of poetry, *Leaves of Grass*, through nine separate editions, seeking respect as a poetic innovator, a teacher, an editor, a printer, a journalist, a novelist, a lecturer, a spokesman against alcoholism, a chronicler of the Civil War, a nurse of wounded soldiers, a famous literary personage in America, hailed in other countries for the power of his words.

With all the astuteness of a 20th-century media manipulator, he had publicized himself, printing a personal letter of praise from Ralph Waldo Emerson without the author's permission, writing excellent reviews of his own book under pseudonyms, petitioning for recognition and public financial support as an unacknowledged genius, standing over the shoulders of friends who wrote about him and directing their words. He had even gone through his papers twice, burning certain ones he did not want to leave behind, those that might detract from the image of Walt Whitman that he had so carefully crafted. To cover his tracks, he had taunted his readers by saying that the real person he was could never be captured in a book:

> When I read the book, the biography famous,
> And is this, then, (said I,) what the author calls a
>   man's life?
> And so will someone, when I am dead and gone, write my
>   life?
> (As if any man really knew aught of my life;
> Why, even I myself, I often think, know little or
>   nothing of my real life;
> Only a few hints—a few diffused, faint clues and
>   indirections I seek for my own use ...)

And he had contradicted himself, as he often did, by claiming at the same time that his poetry was the truth about his experience: "... this is no book, / Who touches this touches a man."

Now, as he was nearing the end of his life, could he throw it all away by openly endorsing the unorthodox sexual conduct that he had written about three decades earlier—even if he did still believe in it? Society considered it an unspeakable perversion. Where would that leave his reputation? He could hide behind his own creativity, knowing that poetry and fiction can reveal an author's thoughts and feelings, yet can never be definitive proof of his actual life. After all, he had created his own literary persona, speaking in the artificially sincere voice of his ideal rather than his real self. His life had become a work of art, his public personality a series of ingenious masks.

Whitman wrote his reply to Symonds with an almost unbelievable intensity:

> —Ab't the questions on Calamus pieces &c: they quite daze
> me.... that the Calamus part has even allow'd the possibility

of such construction as mention'd is terrible—I am fain to hope the pages themselves are not to be even mention'd for such gratuitous and quite at the time entirely undream'd & unreck[on]'d possibility of morbid inferences—wh' are disavow'd by me & seem damnable. Then one great difference between you and me, temperament & theory, is restraint ... My life, young manhood, mid-age, times South, &c: have all been jolly, bodily and doubtless open to criticism—

Tho' always unmarried, I have had six children—two are dead—One living southern grandchild, fine boy, who writes to me occasionally. Circumstances connected with their benefit and fortune have separated me from intimate relations.

I see have written with haste & too great effusion—but let it stand.

Whitman was so upset, that he answered a question Symonds hadn't even asked. His own sexuality was not in question, only his willingness to allow readers to interpret his words in their own way. His defensiveness was transparent. He had spent only a few months in New Orleans when he was in his late twenties, hardly enough time to engender six children—unless he was having affairs with six different women. Of course, no trace has been found of these offspring, but even if he'd fathered 20 children, that would not preclude his endorsement or encouragement of male–male sex. Embarrassingly, he even lied about writing in haste, as an earlier draft of the letter was later found.

Symonds politely replied in a letter addressed to "My dear Master," with thanks that the poet had stated, "so clearly & precisely what you feel about the question I raised." Five years after Whitman's death, however, he published a fuller response:

No one who knows anything about Walt Whitman will for a moment doubt his candour and sincerity. Therefore the man who wrote "Calamus," and preached the gospel of comrade-ship, entertains feelings at least as hostile to sexual inversion as any law-abiding humdrum Anglo-Saxon could desire. (Symonds 97)

Had the master of masks disguised himself so well that he would be remembered as a homophobe rather than as the courageous champion of "the love that dares not speak its name"?

Mercifully, Whitman's talent for contradicting himself was able to save him. As the homosexual identity continued to coa-lesce into a clearly recognized personality type, and as a community of men who loved men began to take shape, Whitman's encouraging words became a beacon for his gay readers, and his lying letter to John Symonds has remained known primarily to scholars rather than the general public, as has an unpublished poem called "Confession and Warning," whose message stands in direct opposition to the brave procla-mations of "Native Moments." In this poem he also identifies himself with society's outcasts, but he expresses a guilty anxiety about those who arouse him:

> What foul thought but I think it?
> What in darkness in bed at night alone or with a com-panion,
>   but that too is mine?
> You prostitutes flaunting over the trottoirs, or obscene in
>   your rooms?
> Who am I that I should call you more obscene than myself?
> ...
> Beneath this impassive face the hot fires of hell
>   continually burn—within me the lurid smutch and
>   the smokes,
> Not a crime can be named but I have it in me waiting,

Lusts and wickedness are acceptable to me,
I walk with delinquents with passionate love.

What were the competing forces in this poetic giant's life that enabled him to set a heroic example for other men who loved men by proclaiming his emergence from the closet into a new community while at the same time feeling ashamed enough to deny this central truth of his life?

two

A Child Went Forth

There was a child went forth every day,
And the first object he look'd upon, that object he became,
And that object became a part of him for the day or
*   a certain part of the day,*
Or for many years or stretching cycles of years.
                              —"There Was a Child Went Forth"

WALT WHITMAN WAS BORN on May 31, 1819 in Hunt-ington, Long Island, thirty miles from New York City. His ancestors were the Dutch Van Velsors on his Quaker mother Louisa's side and the English Whitmans on his father Walter's side. His maternal grandparents lived at Cold Spring, only about a mile from the harbor, and even though Whitman's parents moved to Brooklyn when he was 4 years old, he frequently returned to visit Long Island, where some of his fondest childhood memories were formed.

Whitman's poems about his childhood depict him as an extraordinarily sensitive boy. Spirituality came naturally to him. He went from his grandmother's farm to the beach as often as he could, and there he felt in touch with the world of nature, listening to the ocean's deep bass drum sounds as he followed the undulating white line of foam that separated the sea from the shore. It was there that he first began to contemplate life and death and the soul; and it was there that he first understood that he was to become a poet. In "Out of the Cradle Endlessly Rocking," whose title echoes the rolling rhythm of the sea, he wrote of a young boy who discovers a pair of mockingbirds on the moonlit beach and glories in their love. But when one of them disappears, he is fascinated by the sorrowful song of the survivor:

> Is it indeed toward your mate you sing? or is it
>   really to me?
> For I, that was a child, my tongue's use sleeping, now
>   I have heard you,
> Now in a moment I know what I am for, I awake,
> And already a thousand singers, a thousand songs,
>   clearer, louder and more sorrowful than yours,
> A thousand warbling echoes have started to life within
>   me, never to die.

Then he turns to the sea and listens for an explanation of the
sadness this new awareness has caused him:

> Whereto answering, the sea,
> Delaying not, hurrying not,
> Whisper'd me through the night, and very plainly
>   before daybreak,
> Lisp'd to me the low and delicious word death,
> And again death, death, death, death ...

Of course, Whitman recalled and wrote of these experiences as
an adult, and we must remember as we look to his poetry for an
explanation of his innermost feelings, that they are metaphors
for his actual experience and cannot be accepted as concrete
history.

Although he was a sensitive child, he was not a solitary,
morbid one. He fished for eels in the winter and gathered gull
eggs in the summer with the local boys, but he didn't make any
special friends. Instead, he took great pleasure in the boat
pilots, herdsmen, and fishermen who peopled the seashore, and
whenever possible he visited with them and rode with them on
their boats, exulting in their company, which offered him the
masculine warmth he could not find in his own father.

In "I Sing the Body Electric," Whitman describes an ideal
father, a person not so different from the type of man he
became in his old age (minus the children, of course):

> I knew a man, a common farmer, the father of five
>   sons ...
> This man was of wonderful vigor, calmness, beauty of
>   person,
> The shape of his head, the pale yellow and white of
>   his hair and beard, the immeasurable meaning of his

black eyes, the richness and breadth of his
    manners,
These I used to go and visit him to see, he was wise
    also,
He was six feet tall, he was over eighty years old,
    his sons were massive, clean, bearded, tan-faced,
    handsome,
They and his daughters loved him, all who knew him
    loved him ...

Walter Whitman Sr., unlike this perfect father, was a coarse, cold, irritable man, physically large-boned, tall, and powerful. In "There Was a Child Went Forth," the poet describes what most analysts take to be his own father:

The father, strong, self-sufficient, manly, mean,
    anger'd, unjust,
The blow, the quick, loud word, the tight bargain, the
    crafty lure ...

His father's heroes were the leaders of the American Revolution, and he taught his children the ideas of Thomas Paine, the author of *Common Sense* and *The Age of Reason*, which had applied the theories of logic and science to human affairs in traditional 18th-century fashion: "My country is the world, and my religion is to do good." Paine, like many of the founding fathers, was a Deist, who believed that God had created a mechanical "clockwork" universe and then left it, so that there was no point in personal prayer, and he scoffed at Christian notions of guilt. Following these ideas, Whitman's father practiced no religion, but he did take his children to hear the liberal Quaker preacher Elias Hicks, who defended Paine against his detractors. They probably also heard the early socialist Francis Wright, but neither Whitman nor his father felt a need to join groups. Nonetheless, something was missing for Whitman. "As I Ebb'd with the Ocean of Life" expresses his yearning for closeness with his father (here represented by the land, which abuts the maternal sea):

> I throw myself on your breast my father,
> I cling to you so that you cannot unloose me,
> I hold you so firm till you answer me something.
>
> Kiss me my father,
> Touch me with your lips as I touch those I love ...

Whitman's mother was a small, slim woman with a sweet temper and refined, lady-like manners. Although she was barely literate and could scarcely have understood his writings, she felt closer to her poetic son than to any of her other children. His relationship to her was less complicated than his relationship with his father. They loved and accepted one another gladly. She is described in his poetry as:

> The mother at home quietly placing the dishes on the
>   supper-table,
> The mother with mild words, clean her cap and gown, a
>   wholesome odor falling off her person and clothes
>   as she walks by ...

It was from his mother that Whitman took up the practice of wearing Quaker gray and using in his poems Quaker expressions such as "thou" for "you" and "ninth-month" for "September." For as long as she lived, he remained devoted to her.

Walter and Louisa Whitman had a total of nine children, several of whom suffered physical and psychological ailments. Jesse, the oldest, was eventually committed to an insane asylum. Walter was the second, who looked after the rest when they were young, recording his love for them in a short story called "My Boys and Girls," in which he uses their actual names. Mary Elizabeth grew up to marry a Long Island mechanic. Hanna Louisa, who married an abusive artist named Charles Heyde, moved to Vermont, where her mental state deteriorated from unhappiness to severe neurosis (then called "neuraesthenia"). Next came an infant who lived only a few months and was never named. Andrew Jackson Whitman grew up to become an alcoholic, who married a prostitute; the couple lost a young son under the wheels of a passing carriage. George Washington Whitman married Louisa Orr Haslam, fought in the Civil War, and settled down to run a carpentry shop in Camden, New Jersey. Thomas Jefferson Whitman, Walt's

Walt Whitman Birthplace

The house in which Walt Whitman was born, now a national historic site, was built sometime between 1816 and the time of Whitman's birth in 1819 by Walter Whitman Sr. When the family moved to Brooklyn in 1823, the house was sold to Carlton Jarvis, whose family lived there for much of the 19th century. Historical interest in the house began after a fire in 1910 destroyed much of the kitchen area, and in 1917 the house was purchased by John D. and Georgia Watson. In 1951, the Walt Whitman Birthplace Association acquired the home and in 1957, ownership was taken over by the state of New York, making it the state's 22nd historic site. Much of the house has been restored to it's original condition, and the house remains open to visitors all year round.

favorite sibling, married Martha E. Mitchell, and moved to St. Louis, where he became the superintendent of water works. Eddie, the youngest, was mentally challenged.

Walter Whitman Sr. worked as a builder of houses in Brooklyn, constructing one house and moving his family into it while he went on to build the next. In spite of his pleasant trips to the seashore, the poet later described his boyhood as a restless and unhappy one. One incident became a proud family legend, however. When Whitman was a child, his father took him to see the great French patriot, Lafayette, who had come to George Washington's aid during the Revolution. The Frenchman received an enthusiastic welcome on his visit to New York, and young Walter was one of the few he picked up and kissed on the cheek.

Whitman didn't enjoy his schooling very much. There were few teachers to many pupils, and the teaching was done by rote and regimentation, reinforced with corporal punishment—not much inspiration for a boy who enjoyed letting his mind wander. Whitman was big for his age and bearlike in his movements. Although he was clearly creative, he always felt his mind moved more slowly than he would have liked. He left school at the age of 11, but he enjoyed reading on his own and took pleasure in the stories of the *Arabian Nights* and novels like Sir Walter Scott's *Ivanhoe* and James Fenimore Cooper's *The Last of the Mohicans.* He had no difficulty in learning on his own, admiring science and history, finding them friends rather than enemies of his poetic sensibility.

The series of jobs he began when he was 11 years old violated his sense of freedom, however. He was more a daydreamer than a dedicated worker, so he moved from one job to another, working as a clerk for a lawyer and an office assistant for a doctor and a printer's apprentice for the *Long Island Patriot,* where his first pieces were published when he was only 12 years old.

Brooklyn was still largely rural, so young Walter had plenty of space to indulge his love of solitary walking in his time off. He often found himself down by the docks, where he enjoyed spending time with the men who gathered there to loaf, even though he had to cloak his sensitive, literary nature to be accepted as one of them. He befriended the deckhands on the ferries, who soon were giving him free rides to Manhattan and back.

When his apprenticeship was complete, Whitman got a job as a compositor at a printer's office in Paternoster Row, but in 1835 a great fire there put him and many others out of work, and no new jobs were to be found. His father had moved the family back to his relatives' farm in West Hills, Long Island temporarily, during a slump in the construction business, and in 1836, Whitman, only seventeen years old himself, got a job as a teacher at East Norwich, Long Island. He hated leaving the excitement of the city, and it took him quite a while to readjust to the slow rhythms of country life. By 1838, he had taught in four other towns and over the next few years in half a dozen more, evidently more popular with the students, whom he treated with gentle encouragement, than with their parents or the school administrators.

As a teacher, he was expected to do everything from janitorial tasks in the schoolhouse to sitting up with the dead laid out in their coffins, as well as instructing students. Following local custom, he boarded with the families of his students, often sleeping in the attic with the boys. In one instance, he was asked by an angry farmer to leave because he had evidently grown too attached to the family's son. Another story has circulated in the town of Southold, where the local school, Locust Grove No. 9, was dubbed the "Sodom School" because the teacher was denounced from the pulpit for seducing his students and then tarred and feathered and expelled from the town. A lapse in his writing and a period of depression coincides with the months after this episode, so it is possible that Whitman was the teacher thus punished. (Reynolds, 70-72) The only reference to a comparable event occurs in section 38 of "Song of Myself":

> That I could forget the mockers and insults!
> That I could forget the trickling tears and the blows of the
>   bludgeons and hammers!
> That I could look with a separate look on my own
>   crucifixion and bloody crowning!

Whitman's short stories, which have clear roots in his own experiences and in events he heard about, began to take shape during this period, although many of them were not published until the 1840s. Not particularly original in their form and content, and not especially well written, these stories tend to be simple and sentimental, usually offering clear moral lessons. Many of them concern angry fathers or father figures and their victims, such as "Death in the School-Room (a Fact)," in which a cruel teacher falsely accuses his student of theft and actually beats him to death, and "Bervance: or Father and Son," in which an angry father commits his son to an insane asylum, and "Reuben's Last Wish," in which a child, rendered fatally ill by his father's carelessness, gets him to sign a temperance pledge and then dies.

The mothers in these stories are frequently sweet-tempered widows who dote on their sons. "The Shadow and Light of a Young Man's Soul" is about a young man named Archie Dean, who has to leave the city because he cannot find employment after the great fire on Paternoster Row, which has also destroyed the insurance company which held his widowed mother's money and driven her into poverty. So he is forced to return to

Long Island, where he works as a teacher, and at first he fancies himself too sophisticated for the simple rural people around him until his arrogant sorrows are slowly healed by nature. Finally, inspired by a young woman who works to regain her family's farm and humbled by the death of his young brother, he returns to live with his mother and honor her, and:

> never did his tongue utter words other than kindness, or his lips, whatever annoyances or disappointments came, cease to offer their cheerfullest smile in her presence.

Lest the young Whitman seem too saintly, it should be pointed out that he had his moments of rage. Once, when he was fishing in a pond, a young man named Benjamin Carman began to taunt him by throwing stones. When his boat came close enough, Whitman thrashed the boy with his fishing rod so severely that the boy's father took him to court on an assault charge. (The judge decided in Whitman's favor, saying he hadn't hit Carman hard enough!) Another time, when a church official removed Whitman's hat, Whitman rolled it up and beat the man with it.

But in his stories, saintliness is the norm, even for those who have fallen from grace. An interesting example is "The Child and the Profligate," which was Whitman's most heavily revised story, probably because the original version came too close to the author's true feelings. Once again, his character, a boy of 12 named Charles, is the son of a widowed mother. Lured into a tavern, Charles is harassed by a drunken sailor, who tries to force him to take a drink until a stranger named Langton intercedes. Langton's elegant demeanor sets him apart as a different kind of man from the crude, rustic patrons of the bar:

> His appearance was youthful. He might have been 20-one or

two years old. His countenance was intelligent, and had the air of city life and society. He was dressed not gaudily, but in every respect fashionably; his coat being of the finest broadcloth, his linen delicate and spotless as snow, and his whole aspect that of one whose counterpart may now and then be seen upon the pave in Broadway of a fine afternoon.

The original story describes Langton's sudden rush of feelings for Charles, which is clearly stronger than the paternal feeling that might have been aroused by a young man in distress:

> Why was it that from the first moment of seeing him, the young man's heart had moved with a strange feeling of kindness toward the boy? He felt anxious to know more of him—he felt that he should love him. O, it is passing wondrous, how in the hurried walks of life and business, we meet with young beings, strangers, who seem to touch the fountains of our love, and draw forth their swelling waters. The wish to love and to be loved, which the forms of custom, and the engrossing anxiety for gain, so generally smother, will sometimes burst forth in spite of all obstacles; and, kindled by one, who, till the hour was unknown to us, will burn with a lovely and pure brightness.

In the revised versions of the story, only the first sentence of the above passage was retained, and all of Langton's feelings of burgeoning love are reduced to an instinct toward kindness.

In the original version, after having rescued Charles from the sailor, Langton takes him to sleep in his bed for the night. Whitman describes Langton's lustful thoughts as he lies awake next to the sleeping boy:

> All his imaginings seemed to be interwoven with the youth

who lay by his side; he folded his arms around him, and, while he slept, the boy's cheek rested on his bosom. Fair were those two creatures in their unconscious beauty—glorious, but yet how differently glorious! One of them was innocent and sinless of all wrong: the other—O to that other, what evil had not been present, either in action or to his desires!

Rather than explore the implications of his characters' feelings, Whitman invents a supernatural device in order to forgive Langton for his strange desires:

With one of the brightest and earliest rays of the warm sun, a gentle angel entered his apartment, and hovering over the sleepers on invisible wings looked down with a pleasant smile and blessed them ... Bending over again to the boy's lips, he touched them with a kiss as the languid wind touches a flower ... Now the angel was troubled; for he would have pressed the young man's forehead with a kiss, as he did the child's; but a spirit from the Pure Country, who touches anything tainted by evil thoughts, does it at the risk of having his breast pierced with pain, as with a barbed arrow. At that moment a very pale bright ray of sunlight darted through the window and settled on the young man's features. Then the beautiful spirit knew that permission was granted him: so he softly touched the young man's face with his, and silently wafted himself away on the unseen air.

In the later editions, Charles is simply put to bed in a different room, so there is no longer any need to describe Langton's "evil" thoughts. The angel's troubled thoughts are excised, and his good thoughts are directed to Charles alone. All the versions of the story end with Langton giving up his

drinking and helping to support young Charles and his widowed mother, to the spiritual benefit of all. Finally, in what
seems to be a tacked-on finale, Langton goes on to marry and
raise a family of his own, while always remembering to keep in
touch with Charles.

Although the character of Langton was about the same age
Whitman was when he wrote the story, we cannot say with certainty that Whitman identified himself with the young man
rather than with the boy. It is just as likely that he saw at least
part of the story from Charles's viewpoint, that he dreamed of a
young urbane man who would rescue him from his unexciting
rural life. In his late teens and early twenties, part of him
wanted to protect, and part of him wanted to be protected.
Whatever it may tell us about Whitman's psyche, the story
remains significant for the deletions and alterations we may
trace in its several versions, which at least tell us what Whitman
wanted to say, and perhaps more importantly, what he was not
willing to say.

Whitman's poetry from this period of his late teens and
early twenties gives little indication of the beautiful and strik-
ingly original verses that he would later produce in his thirties.
It is traditionally "sing-song" in its form, maudlin and sentimental in its tone, and didactic or moralistic in its themes,
which include liberty, patriotism, vanity, morality, and death.
He would continue to write about these subjects, but with a
less preachy attitude than we see in "The Love that is Hereafter." When he declares the vanity of human nature—and its
shame about the truth—he might be speaking from his own
experience:

> But man—weak, proud, and erring man,
> Of truth ashamed, of folly vain—
> Seems singled out to know no rest

And of all things that move, feels least
    The sweets of happiness.

Given Whitman's penchant for self-contradiction, it should not be surprising that his mixed feelings about the rural life are at odds with the certainty of his admonition to "Young Grimes" to give up city life in favor of the country:

Leave the wide city's noisy din—
The busy haunts of men—
And here enjoy a tranquil life,
Unvexed by guilt or pain.

It would be another dozen years before his own unique style had matured and he could write from his heart in convincing and elegant verse about his origins, "Starting from Paumanok" (the Indian name for Long Island):

Starting from fish-shape Paumanok where I was born,
Well-begotten, and rais'd by a perfect mother,
After roaming many lands, lover of populous pavements,
Dweller in Manahatta, my city ...
Solitary, singing in the West, I strike up for a New
    World.

Of course, he never roamed in many lands, only in parts of the United States with a brief visit to Canada, but he had a powerful sense of empathy, which broadened his vision and enabled him to see things from the point of view of many kinds of people in many places.

As much as Long Island had provided Whitman with his first sense of self as a boy, it had also felt constrictive when he was a young man eager to explore the variety and excitement of human experience. His mission was to become not only the poet of nature but the poet of the city, and for the rest of his life, he would feel the competing attraction toward both landscapes. By 1841, Whitman was more than ready to return to New York.

chapter
three

Crossing Brooklyn Ferry

I am with you, you men and women of a generation,
  or ever so many generations hence,
Just as you feel when you look on the river and sky, so I felt,
Just as any of you is one of a living crowd, I was one
  of a crowd ...
I too lived, Brooklyn of ample hills was mine,
I too walk'd the streets of Manhattan island, and bathed
  in the waters around it ...
I too had receiv'd identity by my body ...
                    —"Crossing Brooklyn Ferry"

WHITMAN LOVED BEING BACK IN the city, at first appearing as a clean-shaven young man about town, dressed in dapper suits (not unlike those of the urbane character Langton in his story "The Child and the Profligate"), and carrying a walking stick while strolling up Broadway and watching the many kinds of people, wealthy and poor, as they went about their business. The energy of the place invigorated him, but he kept his own peaceful rhythms rather than be forced to rush, even if it meant waiting for the next bus or ferry. He took great pleasure in the company of young omnibus drivers, often riding all the way up and down the street to chat with them and tell them stories while they worked, and they, flattered by the attention of this gentle, intelligent man, welcomed his friendship. On occasion, he even substituted for them when they were ill, being sure to call at their homes to wish them well.

Years later, he would write of the pleasure he took in watching a good-looking young man stride by:

> The expression of a well-made man appears not only in
>   his face,
> It is in his limbs and joints also, it is curiously in
>   the joints of his hips and wrists,
> It is in his walk, the carriage of his neck, the flex
>   of his waist and knees, dress does not hide him,
> The strong sweet quality he has strikes through the
>   cotton and broadcloth,
> To see him pass conveys as much as the best poem,
>   perhaps more,
> You linger to see his back, and the back of his neck
>   and shoulder-side.

For the most part, Whitman made his living as an editor of newspapers while he lived in a series of rooming houses. Before he had left Long Island, he had started a paper himself, *The Long Islander*, but it didn't last very long, so he had secured a job at another paper, *The Long Island Democrat*. Now, in the city, he was able to use his experience to get other jobs, as a printer for *The New World*, as a writer for *The Democratic Review*, and then as an editor for *The Aurora*, *The Evening Tattler*, *The Brooklyn Daily Eagle*, and others. Some of the papers he worked for didn't last very long; others continued, but often did so without him because his work habits were unimpressive. Never a career man, he left the office for hours during the afternoon to pursue his avocations of strolling in the streets, visiting the steambaths, dropping in at a gymnasium, swimming in the East River, and riding the horse-drawn buses and ferries for pleasure.

His editorials began with a series called "Sun-Down Papers From the Desk of a School-Master," which dealt with such subjects as the evil of smoking or the hypocrisy of seemingly good citizens. In the seventh one, fifteen years before the appearance of *Leaves of Grass*, he expressed for the first time his desire to write one great book:

The Great Fire of 1835

Early on in his life Walt Whitman began to learn the trade of printing and in fact worked as a printer until the Great Fire of 1835 devastated the industry along with much of the business district of New York City. On December 16, 1835 a raging fire burned for over 15 hours and destroyed more than 700 buildings. The temperature was reported at 17 degrees below 0 which made it nearly impossible to get water to the blaze. Despite the severe destruction, only two deaths were reported, and in the process of rebuilding, New York developed the Croton Water system, which was one of the most impressive engineering projects of the 19th century.

> I think that if I should make pretentions to be a philosopher, and should determine to edify the world with what would add to the number of these sage and ingenious theories which do already so much abound, I would compose a wonderful and ponderous book. Therein should be treated on, the nature and peculiarities of men, the diversity of their characters, the means of improving their state ... And who shall say that it might not be a very pretty book? Who knows but that I might do something very respectable?

But he confessed the limitations of his knowledge on one significant subject:

> I would carefully avoid saying any thing of woman; because it behooves a modest personage like myself not to speak upon a class of beings of whose nature, habits, notions, and ways he has not been able to gather any knowledge, either by experience or observation.

He wrote descriptions of New York street scenes and people, focusing on the butcherboys, firemen, and horse car drivers who drew his attention. His other editorials dealt with his opinions on many issues. He favored the abolition of capital punishment; he opposed excessive money-making, especially if it came from owning slaves; he supported a living wage for working women and sympathy for unfortunate criminals and prostitutes; he felt that education should be more fully supported and carefully supervised, that the flogging system should be abandoned, and that the curriculum should be based not only on traditions of the past but on the needs of the future democracy. He extolled personal cleanliness, fostered the appreciation of nature, and praised civic and aesthetic improvements in the urban environment.

His enthusiasm for his country was clear when he wrote about his patriotic support of the Union and its grand destiny, his admiration of the free spirit of the West, and his belief that America need no longer imitate the music, art, literature, and manners of Europe, but should be encouraged to believe in the validity of its own culture, an idea sponsored by a literary group that called itself the Young America movement.

One editorial for *The Eagle* contains a commentary on human relationships that must have sounded strange coming from a bachelor:

> If seizing the means of the truest happiness—a home, domestic comfort, children, and the best blessings—be wisdom, then is the unmarried state a great folly. There be some, doubtless, who may not be blamed—whom peculiar circumstances keep in the bands of the solitary; but the most of both sexes can find partners meet for them, if they will.

An undated scrap of manuscript from this period casts a further light on his feelings:

> Why is it that a sense comes always crushing on me as of one happiness I have missed in life? and one friend and companion I have never made?

Wishing to keep up an admirable facade, Whitman did not publish these and other thoughts that revealed his aching loneliness.

In 1842, Whitman wrote his only novel, *Franklin Evans, or The Inebriate: A Tale of the Times By A Popular American Author.* It was a temperance story about a young man from Long Island who goes to New York and marries, but becomes a drunkard and eventually causes the death of his wife. He gives up drinking and heads south, where he marries a Creole woman, but resumes his drinking and falls in love with a blonde widow, eventually causing the deaths of these two women as well. Finally, Evans returns north, where he saves a boy from drowning, which redeems him. He is rewarded with a fortune, and gives up drinking at last. Whitman was not especially proud of this book. He padded it with several stories that he had already written for other publications, and in later years he claimed that he had written it in a few days, locked in a room at Tammany Hall, a political clubhouse, drunk on port and gin cocktails. Since he was never seen drunk in his life and was known to avoid not only alcohol but coffee, tea, and tobacco, it is likely that he was going overboard in his efforts to apologize for the poor quality of the story, which he wrote only for the money he was paid.

From Jean Jacques Rousseau's books, such as *The Social Contract*, Whitman continued his self-education during this period, dropping in at the Egyptian Museum on lower Broadway and holding long conversations with its curator, Dr. Abbott, who encouraged him to continue his reading. Whitman's studies of Egyptology lent much richness to the poetry he would later write, and gave him a sense of the longevity and continuity of human history and culture. He also read books on astronomy that widened his view of the universe, and he began to explore the world of philosophy.

From Jean Jacques Rousseau's books, such as *The Social Contract*, Whitman developed his ideas of the importance of the individual in society and an admiration for the "noble savage" theory, which said that since civilization was an artificial construct, the less "civilized" and more "primitive" people were, the closer they were to the truth of nature, which conferred a certain dignity and innocence on them. From *The Enchyridion* [*Manual*] of Epictetus, he learned the virtue of stoical detachment—that is, the acceptance of life's vicissitudes with equanimity and emotional discipline. From Lucretius' *De Rare Naturum* [*On the Nature of The Universe*] he learned the concept that the spiritual essence inhabits all physical existence, an idea which implies that the body is no less important than the soul.

In Thomas Carlyle's satirical *Sartor Resartus* [*The Tailor Retailored*] Whitman again encountered the idea that the body is the garment of the soul. In Carlyle, he found no admirer of American democracy or of its hero Thomas Paine, but he did find the reestablishment of spirituality that the previous century had abandoned for logic. The creative literature of the Romantic Era, as the early 19th century is known, in its revolt against its predecessors, had replaced logic with intuition as the means to pursue truth. Put another way, they believed that what is real is not what you think, but what you feel.

Whitman was an avid reader of Ralph Waldo Emerson's essays and verse, and in 1842 he attended Emerson's lecture on "The Poet," which called for a sense of wonder in the ordinary rather than strict adherence to traditional forms and meters. It became fashionable in the Romantic era to read Asian religious texts, such as the *Bhagavad Gita*, and through such proponents as Emerson, Hindu and Buddhist cosmology were having a profound effect on American letters in the form of a philosophy called Transcendentalism. Transcendentalists saw the universe as not merely a physical creation, but a spiritual one, in which all life was part of one vast "Oversoul," that was only temporarily separated into individual identities and was restored to the inseparable Whole at death, just as a bucket of water may be drawn from the ocean and may have a separate existence until it is tossed back to become an indistinguishable part of the sea. In other words, the separate bodies in which we appear to exist are only an illusion, since ultimately we are all part of one universal spirit. The body and the soul are one. This concept was to inform Whitman's thinking for the rest of his life.

He went on to read Goethe and Dante and Homer's epics, which he enjoyed reciting loudly to the treetops on his strolls. He went to the theater, preferably by himself, reading Shakespeare's plays carefully before seeing them on the stage, and like many a modern day esthete, he became a great fan of Italian opera, whose music transported him emotionally and had, according to him, a strong effect on his writing style.

In 1848, when he was 28 years old, Whitman was offered the editorship of *The New Orleans Crescent*. By then his family had returned to the city, and he was living with them at home in Brooklyn, so perhaps New Orleans represented a new kind of independence for him. He traveled to Louisiana by stagecoach and riverboat, accompanied by his favorite younger brother Thomas Jefferson Whitman, called "Jeff." The trip was arduous but exciting, and when he arrived, he found himself in a new environment, a southern port city with a strong French cultural influence and easy moral standards, far away from prying eyes, where no one except his innocent young brother knew him.

He and Jeff strolled around the exotic city, observing scenes that Whitman would turn into verbal sketches for the newspaper. In "I Sing the Body Electric" he would later write of seeing a slave auction with what seemed like compassion, but in an abstract, impersonal tone:

Gentlemen look at this curious creature,
Whatever the bids of the bidders they cannot be high
  enough for him,
For him the globe lay preparing quintillions of years
  without one animal or plant,

For him the revolving cycles truly and steadily
  rolled.
In that head the all-baffling brain,
In it and below it the making of the attributes of
  heroes ...

But despite his ability to empathize with everyone, and
despite his poetry and his editorials in support of the down-
trodden, and his rhetoric about the equality of all creatures in
the universe, he did not align himself with the abolitionists
who wanted slavery ended immediately. He sided with the
North during the coming war primarily because he was so
concerned with the preservation and expansion of the American Union.

  Turning inward, he looked—as he always did when he was
alone—to the comfort of Nature, and he later wrote of a
symbol of the comradeship he yearned for:

I saw in Louisiana a live-oak growing,
All alone stood it and the moss hung down from the
  branches,
Without any companion it grew there uttering joyous
  leaves of dark green,
And its look, rude, unbending, lusty, made me think of
  myself,
But I wonder'd how it could utter joyous leaves
  standing alone there without its friend near, for I
  knew I could not,
And I broke off a twig with a certain number of leaves
  upon it ...
Yet it remains to me a curious token, it makes me
  think of manly love ...

Evidently he did find someone to bond with while he was there. "Once I Pass'd Through a Populous City" is a significant poem about New Orleans that reveals both Whitman's nature and his willingness to obscure it. It deals with this relationship:

> Once I pass'd through a populous city imprinting my
>   brain for future use with its shows, architecture,
>   customs, traditions,
> Yet now of all that city I remember only a woman I
>   casually met there who detain'd me for love of me,
> Day by day and night by night we were together—all
>   else has long been forgotten by me,
> I remember I say only that woman who passionately
>   clung to me,
> Again we wander, we love, we separate again,
> Again she holds me by the hand, I must not go,
> I see her close beside me with silent lips sad and
>   tremulous.

Some scholars actually thought that this poem might be proof of the letter he wrote to John Addington Symonds about his six illegitimate children. A photograph of a woman who appeared to be Creole was found tucked into one of his notebooks, and this woman was touted as his New Orleans lover, possibly the mother of his children (but almost certainly not six of them). It wasn't until well after the poet's death that an earlier draft of the poem was discovered, which read:

> Yet now of all that city I remember only a man I
>   casually met there who detain'd me for love of me ...
> I remember I say only that man who passionately clung
>   to me ...

Again he holds me by the hand, I must not go,
I see him close beside me with silent lips sad and
     tremulous.

Whoever this person was, whatever the nature of their relationship, after three months, Whitman returned to New York (with a side trip to the Great Lakes area) full of new potential. Perhaps it was his first sexual relationship, or perhaps it was the first time someone had fallen in love with him. It may even be that it was there that he had a life-altering spiritual experience which he would later write about, but after New Orleans he had a new self-confidence, a new appearance and a new kind of poetry gestating within him.

four

I Celebrate Myself

I celebrate myself and sing myself,
And what I assume you shall assume,
For every atom belonging to me as good belongs to you.
                                                    —"Song of Myself"

FOND OF NEW IDEAS, WHITMAN explored concepts such as Franz Mesmer's "animal magnetism," the study of the physical electromagnetic forces that resulted in sexual appeal or charismatic personality power; hydropathy, the use of water (both internally and externally) to cure ills; and the pseudoscience of phrenology, which purported to delineate character by examining the bumps of the skull on the theory that enlarged areas of the brain corresponded to elevations in the cranium. In 1849, Whitman's phrenological chart was done by Fowler and Wells, who summarized their findings:

> Leading traits of character appear to be Friendship, Sympathy, Sublimity and Self-Esteem, and markedly among his combinations the dangerous faults of Indolence, a tendency to the pleasure of Voluptuousness and Alimentiveness, and a certain reckless swing of animal will ...

Most significant among the long list of traits that were rated were Whitman's high scores in Amativeness (capacity for male–female love) and Adhesiveness (capacity for same-gender love). Their importance lay less in what they may have revealed about the poet's character than in the terminology that gave him a vocabulary for feelings that as yet had to be named in the English language. *Amativeness* parallels the modern term "heterosexuality," and *adhesiveness* parallels the less explicitly sexual term "comradeship," which can, thanks to Whitman's interchanging of the concepts of "friend" and "lover," also be extended to include the modern term "homosexuality."

After editing two more newspapers, *The Daily Eagle* and *The Freeman*, in the 1850s Whitman went to work with his father and his brothers, constructing houses in Brooklyn. Often he dressed in the informal clothes of a carpenter, but in fact he worked on the account books while his father and brothers actually hammered the nails. Although some readers believe he was showing solidarity with the working class, Whitman was not a socialist or trade unionist. It is more likely that he was dressing like the men he found attractive and sought friendships with, hoping to draw closer to them by looking like one of them, a practice called cisvestism. He stopped calling himself by his full name, Walter Whitman Jr., and began to be known as "Walt," even when he signed his writing.

From this time into his old age, many of Whitman's friends commented that he readily drew greetings from the men he passed in the street, whether they actually knew him or not. His beard had grown fuller and made his face seem more handsome, but it was doubtless his penetrating blue-gray eyes that men noticed, eyes that observed the world with a look of saintly compassion and acceptance, and which no doubt lit up with appreciation of manly beauty, wherever he found it. Many men, seeing such approval on a stranger's face might have engaged in an unconscious flirtation, or might have mistaken it for a look of recognition, and thinking they knew their admirer, greeted him as an acquaintance.

Unlike his working-class comrades, however, Whitman continued his love affair with theater and opera. He saw such famous actors as Edwin Booth (whose brother would later assassinate Abraham Lincoln) and such famous sopranos as Jenny Lind, "the Swedish nightingale." In the early 1850s, the Italian soprano Maria Alboni was on tour, and Whitman became her adoring fan, attending every single one of her New York performances. At first he was able to get into many performances free as a newspaper editor, but later he lost that privilege. During the days when he wasn't working with his father, he operated a printing office and stationery store and did some freelance journalism.

Something of lasting importance was also happening during

these years. Whitman began to work seriously on his poetry, gathering phrases, ideas and observations from earlier years, writing rough drafts on the backs of order forms at the newspaper office, and rendering them in a new poetic language—"free verse," which had neither rhyme nor meter. It was a complete break not only from his own earlier, more rigid style, but from the basic traditions of poetry, and it would leave a permanent effect on American poetic form. Where earlier poets had structured their poems carefully with predictable rhythms and rhymes in short and medium length lyrical lines, Whitman created the longest verses yet seen and used the natural rhythms of speech and nature.

He also introduced new perspectives and characters and settings in his poems. Where traditional poets spoke of noble heroes and swooning damsels, Whitman chose the common working people as his characters. And where romantic poets had idealized the bucolic countryside, Whitman became the

Phrenology

Though eventually discredited and termed a pseudoscience, Phrenology was a wide-spread cultural phenomenon in the 19th century. Based on the theories of Franz Joseph Gall, Phrenology, in its most basic form, was the belief that through close examination of the head or skull, one can derive a character profile of the individual. Gall's theories suggested that the mind had distinct faculties, each with its own "organ" in its own location, and that the larger the size of the organ, the more acute the faculty. It has been suggested that throughout the 1840s, Whitman visited phrenological parlors and read phrenology journals including *American Phrenological Journal* published by Fowler and Wells, who later published *Leaves of Grass*.

poet of the city as well as the country. Fond of coining new words, or of borrowing and reshaping words from other languages, he idealized the urban "blab of the pave" and celebrated his freedom as "libertad."

The theme of death remained a poetic standard throughout the century, and we can compare the different ways in which it was handled by Whitman, his predecessors, and his contemporaries. His work was unlike that of the poets of the first half of the century, such as William Cullen Bryant, Ralph Waldo Emerson, Edgar Allan Poe, and Henry Wadsworth Longfellow, all of whom he met during the course of his career.

Bryant's "Thanatopsis" experiments with unrhymed verse, but the rhythm, the vocabulary, and the tone remain formal. In Bryant's poetry, death is treated as an abstract concept:

> Thou shalt lie down
> With patriarchs of the infant world—with kings,
> The powerful of the earth—the wise the good,
> Fair forms, and hoary seers of ages past,
> All in one mighty sepulchre.

Eschewing rhyme and mixing strongly rhythmic lines with less structured ones, Emerson speaks in a wry tone of the dead farmers who once owned the land that now holds them:

> Where are these men? Asleep beneath their grounds:
> And strangers, fond as they, their furrows plow.
> Earth laughs in flowers, to see her boastful boys
> Earth-proud, proud of the earth which is not theirs;
> Who steer the plow, but cannot steer their feet
> Clear of the grave.

As he states in "The Philosophy of Composition," Poe

calculatingly wrote about the deaths of young maidens in order to move his readers. In poems like "The Raven" the striking image of the bird that symbolizes the death of the maiden Lenore is almost trivialized by the overwhelmingly intense internal rhymes and rigid sing-song rhythm of the fictional narrator:

> Then this ebony bird beguiling my sad fancy into
>   smiling,
> By the grave and stern decorum of the countenance it
>   wore,
> "Though thy crest be shorn and shaven, thou," I said,
>   "art sure no craven,
> Ghastly grim and ancient Raven wandering from the
>   nightly shore—
> Tell me what thy lordly name is on the night's
>   Plutonian shore!"
>   Quoth the Raven, "Nevermore."

Longfellow speaks not only of the death of individuals but of whole peoples. In "The Song of Hiawatha" his repetitive rhythms are intended to emulate the sound of Indian drums:

> Ye, who sometimes, in your rambles
> Through the green lanes of the country ...
> Pause by some neglected graveyard
> For a while to muse, and ponder
> On a half-effaced inscription, ...
> Full of all the tender pathos
> Of the Here and the Hereafter;—
> Stay and read this rude inscription,
> Read this Song of Hiawatha!

Emily Dickinson was Whitman's contemporary, but few of her verses were published while she was alive. She, too, wrote about death, but from an original point of view: the voice of the dead person. Her poems are beautifully crafted gems, consisting of a few short lines, carefully rhymed and metered. Her brilliant artistry makes her, with Whitman, one of the two greatest American poets of her century:

> I died for beauty, but was scarce
> Adjusted in the tomb
> When one who died for truth was lain
> In an adjoining room....
>
> And so as kinsmen met a night,
> We talked between the rooms,
> Until the moss had reached our lips
> And covered up our names.

Whitman's view of death is less formal and reverent than that of the poets who preceded him. Where Bryant and Emerson spoke of death as the leveler of human society, and Poe and Longfellow spoke of it as a gloomy specter that haunts our lives, Whitman faced it with bright exultation as a natural part of existence. His relationship to death is as intimate as Dickinson's, but he does not share her quiet resignation. Rather, he embraces and celebrates death as a part of the transcendental cycle of life. In "Song of Myself," he states, "And to die is different from what anyone supposed, and luckier." Later in "When Lilacs Last in the Dooryard Bloom'd," he exclaims:

> Prais'd be the fathomless universe,
> For life and joy, and for objects and knowledge
>   curious,

And for love, sweet love—but praise! praise!
  praise!
For the sure-enwinding arms of cool-enfolding death.

This celebration of death is woven throughout his work. Whitman opted neither for the sentimentality of his predecessors nor for the delicate beauty of Dickinson, but for a poetry of positivism and gusto shaped by his inner voice. His verses were an expansion of the Romantic concept of "organic form," which stipulated that the form and rhythm of a poem should be adapted to the contents (that is, the poet's thoughts and feelings) rather than having the message adapted to fit a preconceived rhyme and meter.

In order to bring his feelings to life, Whitman established what seemed like a direct voice through which he established an intimacy with his reader. This seemingly direct autobiographical voice was, however, a masterpiece of fictional invention. The ruggedly barbaric natural man he invented existed more in his fantasies than in reality, where he was a burly but gentle man of letters. So enticingly genuine was his fictional creation that he actually uses it to seduce his readers sexually. In "Whoever You Are Holding Me Now in Hand," he speaks of his book as if it were his body, which seems unborn or dead when it is merely lying in the library:

But just possibly with you on a high hill, first
  watching lest any person for miles around approach
  unawares,
Or possibly with you sailing at sea, or on the beach
  of the sea or some quiet island,
Here to put your lips upon mine I permit you,
With the comrade's long-dwelling kiss or the new
  husband's kiss,

For I am the new husband and I am the comrade.

Or if you will, thrusting me beneath your clothing,
Where I may feel the throbs of your heart or rest upon
   your hip,
Carry me when you go forth over land or sea;
For thus merely touching you is enough, is best,
And thus touching you would I silently sleep and be
   carried eternally.

Again in "So Long," he announces that the reader is not
holding a book but a man, and that man is a lover:

(Is it night? are we here together alone?)
It is I you hold and who holds you,
I spring from the pages into your arms—decease
   calls me forth
O how your fingers drowse me,
Your breath falls around me like dew, your pulse lulls
   the tympans of my ears,
I feel immerged from head to foot,
Delicious, enough....

Dear friend whoever you are take this kiss,
I give it especially to you, do not forget me.

This level of intimacy with the reader is unparalleled and has
created a cult following of readers who speak of being in love
with this poet. He leaves his readers not only with the beauty of
his words, but with a philosophy and a cosmology, a framework
within which to experience their lives.

   Whitman's *Leaves of Grass* first appeared in 1855, and
although like most innovative works it was received with mixed

reactions, it became the single most influential book of poems in the history of American literature. The 1850s has been called the "American Renaissance" because aside from *Leaves of Grass*, it saw the publication of Hawthorne's *The Scarlet Letter*, Melville's *Moby Dick*, and Thoreau's *Walden*, and at last American literature, which had long been considered provincial and inferior, was in full flower.

The first edition of *Leaves of Grass* was a slim, dark green volume, printed by the Rome Brothers of Brooklyn, containing a preface, 12 untitled poems, and several articles and reviews. Imprints of leaf patterns adorned its leather cover, and the title appeared in gold letters decorated with roots and leaves. Its title is a play on words, since the normal phrase is "blades" of grass. "Leaves" suggests the pages of a book, and "grass" is also a printer's term for trial pages that are thrown away, as if the carefully revised poems inside were temporary sketches, Whitman's effort to suggest modesty because he knew he would be accused of egotism for daring to make himself the subject of his own poetry. The cover and title page made no mention of the author.

The frontispiece was another break with tradition. Although authors had traditionally been represented by lithographs of themselves posed carefully in formal dress, Whitman used a drawing of himself by Gabriel Harrison, which shows him slouching with one hand on his hip and the other in his pocket. He's wearing a tilted hat and an open-collared shirt that shows the top of his long underwear. Although he is only 35 years old, there is gray in his beard. The look in his eyes is a cool, steady gaze, almost daring the reader to engage him.

Many of Whitman's prose works have a dense, turgid style, but the Preface to the first edition of *Leaves of Grass* has passages that have such lyrical phrase lengths and cadences that they have successfully been turned into poetry. Here we see the first appearance of a technique that would remain a feature of both his poetry and prose: the lengthy "catalogue" or list of examples, an effort to include as many trees or rivers or types of people in his writing as possible, since his spiritual empathy relates all of them to one another. His themes include the ideas that evolved from his earlier reading and discussions: the justification of American culture as independent from its European predecessors, the relationship of the body to the soul, the value of stoical detachment from events, the beauty of unadorned, natural language, and the importance of democracy as a community of "Supremes," in which everyone's vision is valid and equal.

Most of the 1855 Preface, building upon Emerson's lecture on poetry, deals with the role of the American poet, who is to bring together the people's views and inspire them to action, to offer his sense of wonder as a new eyesight for his readers, to proclaim the natural state of liberty and the oneness of all things in nature. The test of a great poet, he believed, was the universality of his message, and the proof of such a poet is that he would be absorbed into his country's culture. Ultimately, in Whitman's theory, the American poet was to replace the priest as the spiritual leader of a new age, teaching that it is the individual rather than the institution of the church that is holy. As evidence of his own candidacy to be this new kind of spiritual leader, he offered the following advice:

> This is what you shall do: Love the earth and sun and the animals, despise riches, give alms to every one that asks, stand up for the stupid and crazy, devote your income and labor to others, hate tyrants, argue not concerning God, have patience and indulgence toward the people, take off your hat to nothing known or unknown or to any man or number of

men, go freely with powerful uneducated persons and with the young and with the mothers of families, read these leaves in the open air every season of every year of your life, re-examine all you have been told at school or church or in any book, dismiss whatever insults your own soul, and your very flesh shall be a great poem and have the richest fluency not only in its words but in the silent lines of its lips and face and between the lashes of your eyes and in every motion and joint of your body.

In some ways, he hoped that his book of poems would be received as a new Bible. The 19th century produced a number of books with that ambition, not least among them Carlyle's *Sartor Resartus*, one of the stronger influences among Whitman's readings.

The primary poem in Whitman's book eventually grew to a length of nearly 50 pages in the course of its many editions. It was later titled "Song of Myself," but the earliest version is widely considered to have the most vitality and immediacy. It is Whitman's single most important work, and it deserves close scrutiny. We will examine only some of the wealth of themes and images that appear in it. His opening lines (quoted at the beginning of this chapter) have often been attacked for sounding egotistical and were an affront to the Victorian sensibility that prized modesty (even false modesty). But when Whitman says he celebrates himself, he is clearly doing so in the name of everyone connected to that self via the Oversoul. Although he is one man, he represents not only himself, but all Americans, all humanity, even all of the universe. He identifies himself with everyone from the hounded runaway slave to Christ crucified. His physical identity is considered separately from his spiritual identity, or soul:

> I loafe and invite my soul,
> I lean and loafe at my ease.... observing a spear
>   of summer grass.

Much of the rest of the poem might be seen as what he observes in this blade of grass, which represents an individual life separated from the collective lawn from which it was plucked, just as the individual soul is separated from the Over-soul. The grass becomes a symbol of life growing from death:

> A child said, What is the grass? fetching it to me
>   with full hands:
> How could I answer the child?.... I do not know
>   what it is any more than he....
>
> I guess it is the handkerchief of the Lord,
> A scented gift and remembrancer designedly dropped,
> Bearing the owner's name someway in the corners, that
>   we may see and remark, and say Whose?
>
> Or I guess the grass is itself a child.... the
>   produced babe of the vegetation....
>
> And now it seems to me the beautiful uncut hair
>   of graves.
> Tenderly will I use you curling grass,
> It may be you transpire from the breasts of young men,
> It may be if I had known them I would have loved them ...
>
> The smallest sprout shows there is really no death ...

Like the grass, any human being is of inestimable significance, and the declaration of this belief was not meant to sound egotistical:

I am an acme of things accomplished, and I an encloser
of things to be.

Circling around to the same themes again and again, much
of the poem deals with the reality of the physical body, which
in his era was traditionally either idealized as a temple of the
spirit or considered a source of shame:

Welcome is every organ and attribute of me, and of
any man hearty and clean,
Not an inch nor a particle of an inch is vile, and
none shall be less familiar than the rest.

Rather than dragging the soul down to the level of the body, he
elevated the body to the level of the soul. An old tradition in
poetry stages a dialogue between the body and soul. Whitman
takes this notion one step further and, shockingly, has the soul
make love to the body in the key fifth section of "Song of
Myself":

I believe in you my soul…. the other I am [i.e.,
his body] must not abase itself to you,
And you must not be abased to the other….

I mind how we lay in June, such a transparent summer
morning;
You settled your head athwart my hips and gently
turned over upon me,
And parted the shirt from my bosom-bone, and plunged
your tongue to my barestript heart,
And reached till you felt my beard, and reached till
you held my feet.

The position he carefully delineates suggests the sexual practice of fellatio, sometimes practiced by women on men but often associated with male–male love—an intriguing choice to show the relation between body and soul. It is possible that he was encoding an actual physical experience, or that he is describing what is now called an "out-of-body experience" in which an image of the self separates from the physical self; but nowhere in the annals of this "astral projection" is there an instance of sex between two parts of the same self. At the very least, this suggestion of oral sex is a brilliant new poetic image for the integration of two selves or two aspects of the same self into one, but even more important are the lines that follow:

> Swiftly arose and spread around me the peace and joy
>   and knowledge that pass all the art and argument of
>   the earth;
> And I know that the hand of God is the elderhand of my
>   own,
> And I know that the spirit of God is the eldest
>   brother of my own,
> And that all the men ever born are also my brothers....
>   and the women my sisters and lovers,
> And that a kelson [foundation] of the creation is love ...

In the juxtaposition of these two passages, we see a central element of Whitman's sensibility, perhaps the experience that unleashed his newly impassioned poetic force. The sexual union not only represents a spiritual experience, it actually triggers an instance of "cosmic consciousness," or mystical awareness, the spontaneous and immediate sense of the indissoluble unity not only of momentary lovers but of all eternal creation.

The mystical awareness is not necessarily connected with established religion. Whitman, depicting himself as the new American poet-priest, speaks with some condescension to the clergy and declares that his direct religious experience needs no intermediary:

Divine am I inside and out, and I make holy whatever I
   touch or am touched from;
The scent of these arm-pits is aroma finer than
   prayer,
This head is more than churches or bibles or creeds.
If I worship any particular thing it shall be some of
   the spread of my body ...

This body, as a representative of the cosmic self, enlarges to fill the world:

Swift wind! Space! My Soul! Now I know it is true what
   I guessed at ...
My ties and ballasts leave me.... I travel....
   I sail.... my elbows rest in the sea-gaps,
I skirt the sierras.... my palms cover continents,
I am afoot with my vision.

It is important to remember when we turn our focus to Whitman's spiritual side that his mysticism is part of a long tradition of homosexual spirituality. In many tribes the shaman or medicine man was a man who had sex with other men. The *berdache* tradition of the American Indian tribes exemplifies this linkage of homoeroticism and mysticism or magic. Whitman returns again and again to the erotic:

Through me forbidden voices,

> Voices of sexes and lusts.... voices veiled, and I
>   remove the veil,
> Voices indecent by me clarified and transfigured.

He describes a ride on a stallion with suggestions of coupling with a male lover, and he similarly makes love to the earth and the sea and the night. Over and over, Whitman describes attractive workingmen: an African-American cart driver, his muscles and crisp hair burnished by the sun; the butcher-boy removing his blood-stained apron; the blacksmith with his begrimed hairy chest; as well as the farmboy, the mechanic, the hunter, and the woodsman. All are ennobled by his erotic vision. In one passage, he looks through the eyes of a woman who watches 28 naked young men bathing in a river and imagines herself stroking them, and being showered with their "spray." No fantasy or act is shameful. All sex is divine.

Finally, this intertwining of body and soul, sex and spirit, must come to its mortal end. As his decline begins, Whitman assumes the role of teacher, taking his reader by the hand to guide him to the road that awaits. His message is clear and direct:

> I have said that the soul is not more than the body,
> And I have said that the body is not more than the
>   soul,
> And nothing, not God, is greater to one than one's
>   self is.
> And whoever walks a furlong without sympathy walks to
>   his own funeral, dressed in his shroud.

The body and soul that comprise the self are both of supreme importance—and so is every other self. It is love of one's fellow human, then, rather than self-love that is the key to "Song of

Myself," and as the poem closes, many of Whitman's admirers realize that they feel real grief for him. As the sun sets and the last clouds of day wait for him, he is ready to leave us at last:

> I depart as air.... I shake my white locks at the
> runaway sun,
> I effuse myself in eddies and drift it in lacy jags.
>
> I bequeath myself to the dirt to grow from the grass I
> love,
> If you want me again look for me under your bootsoles....
> Failing to fetch me at first keep encouraged,
> Missing me one place search another,
> I stop some where waiting for you.

Whitman told Ralph Waldo Emerson that he printed 1,000 copies of the first edition of *Leaves of Grass* and that they readily sold, but in spite of all his self-promotion, that was apparently not the case. No one knows what became of the many unsold copies.

Visitors to Whitman's tomb in Harleigh Cemetery, Camden, New Jersey, will be disappointed to find that he is not beneath their bootsoles. He is buried in an above-ground crypt with five other members of his family. But the lovely poetic image remains, and legions of Whitman's followers draw sustenance from his words whenever they set foot on the grass.

five

The Love of Comrades

*I will plant companionship thick as trees along all
the rivers of America, and along the shores of the
great lakes, and all over the prairies,
I will make inseparable cities with their arms about
each other's necks,
   By the love of comrades,
     By the manly love of comrades.*

— "For You, O Democracy"

A WEEK AFTER THE PUBLICATION of *Leaves of Grass* Walter Whitman Sr. died. Although he would write years later of the death of his "dear father," there is no evidence that the poet was devastated by the loss. It was on his mother that Walt and his brothers and sisters most depended. After a short period in which most of the family gathered to mourn, everyone returned to his or her normal business.

Whitman continued to promote his new book. In a Springfield, Illinois law office Abraham Lincoln heard a discussion of the radical poetry and took the book to his desk for half an hour, after which he exclaimed that aside from a few indelicate references, he found the writing virile, fresh, unique, and unconventional and thought that it showed promise for a new kind of poetry. He took the book home one evening, but brought it back the next day, saying that he had barely rescued it from being "purified by fire" by his wife. Lincoln asked that the book be left out on a table in the office, and he often read aloud from it. But *Leaves of Grass* was not always rescued. Offended by its rude physicality, other people, including the poet John Greenleaf Whittier, actually did burn the volume. Emily Dickinson, hearing of its vulgarity, simply refused to read it.

At the end of 1855, Ralph Waldo Emerson paid the first of several visits to Whitman in New York. On one visit, Emerson took him to dinner at a hotel, after which Whitman took the proper New Englander out for an evening at the Firemen's Hall, which was full of the rowdy working men whom Whitman loved. Predictably, Emerson found the experience entirely distasteful, too coarse for his more delicate sensibilities.

Whitman continued to exult in the appearance and manners of working-class men and boys, and he began to enter long lists of scores of their names in his notebooks. It is highly doubtful that he had sexual contact with so many people, so his reasons

for listing them are unclear. He may have wanted to refer to
them in his poems, or perhaps they were men he hoped to
know better, and the lists were a way of remembering their
names. In a few cases, he gave them Christmas presents of
gloves or shirts. Some names were there for practical reasons, so
he would know whom to call upon to get work done. Most
likely, however, he simply wanted to "collect" them, to possess
the male beauty he had encountered, at least in memory. Sometimes the lists are scant reminders, as in the following selection:

{3} Hank Pierce (4th av [probably an omnibus route]
Charley (black hair & eyes—round face) 4th av.
Albert, (Mrs. Jones's son)
Jack (—4th av.—now in a N.Y. Express wagon
Frank (Beeswax) [a nickname]
Anson W. Turner (oyster Fulton Market)
Charles Brown (Broadway Brownie)
Storrs King (or "Fulton" with Jack Garrison
John Schoonmake (Lawyer around City Hall remember Ben
  Carman [a reference to the Long Island boy Whitman
  thrashed with a fishing rod]
Jakey (James) tall, genteel friend of Brownie)
Jay (5th av.)—19
Bill—(big, black round eyes, large coarse ...
John Campbell, round light complex lymphatic,
  good-look
John (light complex—light gray eyes, light hair
{4} Edward Smithson (20) full-eyed genteel boy I meet
  often at the ferries—Irish or English ...
Bob Fraser (28) policeman (5–6), slow, mild Cor Myrtle
  & Raymond
Tom Haynes (26) driver, Myrtle-mild—
August (Gus) Dutch boy (16) with cake

The list goes on for another dozen pages.

At other times, he gave much fuller data:

> Peter—large, strong-boned youn[g] fellow, driver.— Should weigh 180. Free and candid to me the very first time he saw me.—Man of strong self-will, powerful coarse feelings and appetites—had a quarrel,—borrowed $300—left his father's, somewhere in the interior of the state—fell in with a couple of gamblers—hadn't been home or written there in seven years.—I liked his refreshing wickedness ...
>
> George Fitch.—Yankee boy—Driver.—Fine nature, amiable, of sensitive feelings, a natural gentleman—of quite a reflective turn. Left his home because his father was perpetually "down on him."—When he told me of his mother, his eyes watered.—Good looking, tall, curly haired, black-eyed fellow, age about 23 or 4—slender face with a smile— trousers tucked in his boots—cap with the front-piece turned behind.—
>
> *Bloom.*—Broad-shouldered, six-footer, with a hare-lip.— Clever fellow, and by no means bad looking.—(George Fitch has roomed with him a year, and tells me there is no more honorable man breathing.) ...
>
> *Aaron B. Cohn*—talk with—he was from Fort Edward Institute—appears to be 19 years old—fresh and affectionate young man—spoke much of a young man named *Gilbert L. Bill* (of Lyme, Connecticut) who thought deeply about Leaves of Grass, and wished to see me.

In 1855 and 1856, Whitman returned to journalism, writing in *Life Illustrated,* a magazine published by his phrenologist friends Fowler and Wells. Not surprisingly, a number of favorable articles about *Leaves of Grass* appeared in this magazine, some of them likely influenced if not written by

Whitman himself. He also wrote a zealous piece called "The Eighteenth Presidency" opposing the extension of slavery into the new territories, but supporting the complete end of slavery only by a change in the Constitution. The piece was set in type but never published, perhaps because it didn't quite agree with any one political party's view, yet the time was coming when every citizen would have to take a stand on ending all slavery, an issue which was threatening to tear the nation in half.

During 1856, Whitman prepared the second edition of *Leaves of Grass*. The size and shape of the book changed from a large-paged, thin, flat volume to a pocket-sized, small-paged, thick one. Included in the volume (and perhaps printed in some late issues of the first edition) is a letter from Ralph Waldo Emerson, New England's leading literary figure, who had been sent a paper-bound version before the final hardcover edition came out. The letter reads, in part:

> I am not blind to the worth of the wonderful gift of "*Leaves of Grass.*" I find it the most extraordinary piece of wit and wisdom that America has yet contributed.... I give you joy of your free and brave thought.... I greet you at the beginning of a great career ... I wish to see my benefactor and have felt much like striking my tasks and visiting New York to pay you my respects.

As enthusiastic as Emerson was, he grew quite angry when he learned that Whitman had printed his letter in the hardbound edition without his permission, and it was a while before the men actually did meet.

Other articles include some general material about the state of contemporary poetry, and a biographical sketch of the author, which describes him as:

a person singularly beloved and welcomed, especially by young men and mechanics—one who has firm attachments there, and associates there—one who does not associate with literary and elegant people—one of the two men sauntering along the street with their arms over each others' shoulders, his companion some boatman or shipjoiner, or from the hunting tent or lumber-raft ...

Some of the articles are signed, and some are not, but judging by their style, content, and tone, several of them are most likely by Whitman himself. One, borrowing some language from the poetry in the book, portrays the public persona he has invented:

An American bard at last! One of the roughs, large, proud, affectionate, eating, drinking, and breeding, his costume manly and free, his face sunburnt and bearded, his postures strong and erect, his voice bringing hope and prophecy to the generous races of young and old. We shall cease shamming and be what we really are. We shall start an athletic and defiant literature....

The original 12 poems from the first edition were supplemented by a number of new poems, which would later be given the familiar titles with which they have endured as classics. Among the poems were "Sun-Down Poem," later called "Crossing Brooklyn Ferry," in which he turns a short ferry trip into a spiritual journey through time; "Poem of Many in One," later known as "By Blue Ontario's Shore," which incorporates 60 lines from the 1855 Preface; and "Poem of the Road," which later became "Song of the Open Road," in which he proclaims the virtue of the restless American spirit and his attachment to other travelers through life:

What is it I interchange so suddenly with strangers?
What with some driver as I ride on the seat by his
  side?
What with some fisherman, drawing his seine by the
  shore, as I walk by and pause?

The answer, probably, is an erotic attraction, which was beginning to grow more and more manifest in his poetry. A poem originally called "Bunch Poem," later called "Spontaneous Me," innocently begins with an excursion into the countryside:

Spontaneous me, Nature,
The loving day, the mounting sun, the friend I am
  happy with,
The arm of my friend hanging idly over my shoulder ...

Poetry itself is represented by male genitals:

The poems of the privacy of the night, and of men like
  me,
This poem drooping shy and unseen that I always carry,
  and that all men carry,
(Know once and for all, avow'd on purpose, wherever
  are men like me, are our lusty lurking masculine
  poems.)

Finally this poem goes daringly farther than any other and explicitly describes a young man masturbating:

The sensitive, orbic, underlapp'd brothers,
  that only privileged feelers may be intimate where
  they are,

The curious roamer the hand roaming all over the body,
  the bashful withdrawing of flesh where the fingers
  soothingly pause and edge themselves,
The limpid liquid within the young man,
The vex'd corrosion so pensive and so painful,
The torment, the irritable tide that will not be at
  rest ...
The young man that wakes deep at night, the hot hand
  seeking to repress what would master him,
The mystic amorous night, the strange half-welcome
  pangs, visions, sweats,
The pulse pounding through palms and trembling
  encircling fingers, the young man all color'd, red,
  ashamed, angry;
The souse upon me of my lover the sea, as I lie
  willing and naked ...

(Note the revealing sudden shift from "the young man" to "me.")

The inevitable counterpart of sex in much of Western litera-ture is death. Another poem introduced in 1856 was first called "Poem of Wonder at the Resurrection of the Wheat," later re-titled "This Compost." A century and a half later, it has a striking resonance in the age of AIDS:

O how can it be that the ground itself does not
  sicken? ...
Are they not continually putting distemper'd corpses
  within you? ...
What chemistry!
That the winds are not really infectious,
That this is no cheat, this transparent green-wash of
  the sea which is so amorous after me,

Whitman on Whitman

Walt Whitman knew that if his book was going to reach the public he loved and embraced in his poems, it would be necessary to take some care of its reception. Serving as his own critical "Kosmos," Whitman anonymously celebrated himself and sang himself with his characteristic gusto in reviews in three different papers: the *United States Review*, the *Brooklyn Daily Times*, and the *American Phrenological Journal*.

Some of the self-confidence evident in the reviews must have been inspired by Ralph Waldo Emerson's high praise of *Leaves* in a July 1855 letter to Whitman. "I find it the most extraordinary piece of wit and wisdom that America has yet contributed. I am very happy in reading it, as great power makes us happy," wrote Whitman's hero: "I greet you at the beginning of a great career." Understandably proud, Whitman saw to it that the letter got printed in the New York *Tribune*, though he conveniently neglected to secure Emerson's consent. Interestingly, Whitman's own reviews affirmed what many of his critics asserted *against* him. The "author" was "one of the roughs, large, proud, affectionate, eating, drinking, and breeding, his costume manly and free, his face sunburnt and bearded ...," he wrote of himself in the *United States Review*. "Politeness this man has none, and regulation he has none," he wrote in the Brooklyn *Times*. Of course, in Whitman's book, these qualities are virtues, not vices. If *Leaves of Grass* gave evidence of "New York rowdyism," as one reviewer complained, Whitman was happy to turn the idea around and accept the critique as a compliment. One of the roughs himself, he knew what the roughs really wanted, opinions of all predictably ruffled reviewers notwithstanding: "Where are the gristle and beards, and broad breasts, and space and ruggedness, and nonchalance, that the souls of the people love?" he ambitiously asked of the whole American literary tradition in the *United States Review*.

That it is safe to allow it to lick my naked body all
  over with its tongues,
That it will not endanger me with the fevers that have
  deposited themselves in it,
That all is clean forever and forever ...
That when I recline on the grass I do not catch any
  disease,
Though probably every spear of grass rises out of what
  was once a catching disease ...

In the same year that the second edition appeared, Whitman received a visit from two esteemed literary figures, probably sent by Emerson. Bronson Alcott was the father of the writer Louisa May Alcott, and Henry David Thoreau was the author of "Civil Disobedience" and *Walden*, both of which championed the rights of the individual. They came to Whitman's house in Brooklyn and were surprised not to be received in a parlor, but in the poet's attic bedroom, where a chamberpot was plainly visible beneath the unmade bed in which he slept with his mentally challenged younger brother Eddie. Three unframed homoerotic pictures adorned the wall: one of the hero Hercules; one of Bacchus, the Greek God of revelry; and one of Silenus, a lusty, goat-footed satyr.

Alcott recorded in his journal that he was impressed by the poet's working-class clothes, consisting of an open-breasted shirt revealing a red flannel undershirt, coarse overalls, a striped calico jacket with a collar like the poet Lord Byron's, cowhide boots and a heavy large-pocketed coat, calling the look an "example to all men hereafter." The visitor was struck by Whitman's gray eyes, cautious yet wise, and his slow manner, resting his head on a pillow as he sat on the couch and listened carefully, asking the speaker to repeat anything he didn't catch the first time, openly stating in a voice that was "deep, sharp, tender sometimes and almost melting," that he was lazy; but he was clearly interested in everything. He was, however, most interested in himself, Alcott found, calling the poet an egotist who couldn't abide a conversation for very long if he wasn't noted in it, but he later noted that if Whitman's arrogance were cured, "good may come, and great things, of him." (Allen, 202, 204)

The poet's mother added to the portrait by describing his syncopated comings and goings, his complete disregard of the schedule of meals in the house, arriving for breakfast whenever he had a mind to and leaving for a walk just as the table was being set for dinner. (Allen, 203) Evidently she indulged him in his independence, perhaps awed by his literacy and that of his well-groomed guests.

Thoreau concluded in a letter to a friend that although Whitman was peculiar and rough in his exterior, the poet was "essentially a gentleman." After reading the second edition of *Leaves of Grass*, he called Whitman "the most interesting fact to me at present." He said that the poetry might turn out to be less sensual than it appeared, and if people were offended by what they saw in it (probably a reference to the masturbation sequence in "Bunch Poem"), that could only be because it reminded them of their own experience. All in all, he found the poetry "very brave & American" and commented, "He is probably the greatest democrat the world has seen ... He occasionally suggests something a little more than human." As to Whitman's reputation for arrogance, Thoreau concluded:

> We ought to rejoice in him. He occasionally suggests something a little more than human.... Since I have seen him, I find that I am not disturbed by any brag or egotism in his book. He may turn out to be the least of a braggart of all, having a better right to be confident, (Allen, 204–205)

The second edition of *Leaves of Grass* did not sell enough copies to make any profit, and after a few months, it was no longer advertised. Whitman worked only occasionally for *The Brooklyn Times*, but he was not making enough money to sustain himself. He borrowed $200 from a friend, then had to face a lawsuit when he was unable to pay it back and was forced to give up some of his books and pictures to his debtor.

In his spare time, he frequented Pfaff's Tavern, in what is now called the SoHo district of Manhattan. Pfaff's was a gathering place for the artistic bohemian crowd, especially for writers, and probably for men attracted to other men, who found the denizens of such an environment more tolerant of their manners. Although the place was loud and somewhat raucous, Whitman was observed to sit quietly sipping his drink amid the din. Occasionally he borrowed small amounts of money to pay for his drinks, but he always repaid it without delay.

In the late 1850s, when Whitman was in his late thirties, an athletic young man in his late teens named Fred Vaughan came to board with the Whitmans. Their relationship set the pattern for Whitman's later relationships with younger men. Whitman became the father figure: the mentor, adviser, and daily companion who helped Fred to get employment; and Fred became the son: eager for the older man's company and guidance, not quite certain of the reason for their attachment, but glad of it.

The Boston publishers Thayer and Eldridge wrote to Whitman early in 1860 with great enthusiasm, expressing their sense of kinship with his ideals and offering to make money for them all by promoting a third edition of *Leaves of Grass*. Their eagerness to see any new poems he might have written may well have been the inspiration for including the "Calamus" and "Children of Adam" poems, which may be called some of America's greatest love poetry. The urgency of their appeal suggests that they, too, knew something about manly comradeship:

> When a man dares to speak his thought in this day of refinement—so called—it is difficult to find his mates to act amen to it. Now we want to be known as the publishers of Walt Whitman's books and put our name as such under his, on title pages ...
>
> We are young men. We "celebrate" ourselves by acts. Try us....
>
> Fraternally yours,
Thayer & Eldridge

Whitman agreed to the new edition, which was published at the end of 1860 with a new frontispiece. It also featured a more traditionally decorous engraving taken from a painting by Charles Hine, showing the hatless poet, neatly groomed, with his necktie tied in a loose bow around his open-collared shirt, which is covered with a jacket. The look in his eye is distant, almost yearning.

Whitman's involvement with Fred Vaughan was most likely the source of the feelings in many of the newly included poems of the third edition of *Leaves of Grass* in 1860. There is insufficient data to determine whether their relationship was physically consummated, but if we use the poetry as evidence, some of their feelings seem clear. In "Earth, My Likeness" we see that Whitman passionately desired Fred:

> For an athlete is enamour'd of me, and I of him,
> But toward him there is something fierce and terrible
>   in me eligible to burst forth,
> I dare not tell it in words, not even in these songs.

In "We Two Boys Together Clinging," he exuberantly wrote of
his fantasies of ideal comradeship:

> We two boys together clinging,
> One the other never leaving,
> Up and down the roads going, North and South
>   excursions making,
> Power enjoying, elbows stretching, fingers clutching,
> Arm'd and fearless, eating, drinking, sleeping,
>   loving,
> No law less than ourselves owning ...

In "We Two, How Long We Were Fool'd," he extends his love
to all nature, immortalizing it:

> We are bedded in the ground, we are rocks,
> We are oaks, we grow in the openings side by side,
> We browse, we are two among the wild herds,
>   spontaneous as any,
> We are two fishes swimming in the sea together ...
> We are two predatory hawks, we soar above and look
>   down,
> We are two resplendent suns ... we are as two comets ...
> We are seas mingling, we are two of those cheerful
>   waves rolling over each other and interwetting each
>   other ...
> We have voided all but freedom and all but our own
>   joy.

One poem, "When I Heard at the Close of the Day," suggests that they did make love, or at least that they shared the
same bed, and that no amount of success and fame could equal
the pleasure of being intimate with his loving comrade:

> For the one I love most lay sleeping by me under the
>   same cover in the cool night,
> In the stillness in the autumn moonbeams his face was
>   inclined toward me,
> And his arm lay lightly around my breast—and that
>   night I was happy.

He openly taunts the reader, suggesting that he is "far different from what you suppose" in "Are You the New Person Drawn toward Me?":

> Do you think it is so easy to have me become your
>   lover? ...
> Do you suppose yourself advancing on real ground
>   toward a real heroic man?
> Have you no thought O dreamer that it may be all ...
>   illusion?

He wrote of his fear of failure in "Recorders Ages Hence," significantly equating "friends" with "lovers" and describing himself as someone:

> Who often walk'd lonesome walks thinking of his dear
>   friends, his lovers,
> Who pensive away from one he lov'd often lay sleepless
>   and dissatisfied at night,
> Who knew too well the sick, sick dread lest the one he
>   lov'd might secretly be indifferent to him ...

And finally in "Hours Continuing Long, Sore and Heavy-Hearted," he wrote of his bitter disappointment and anguish:

> Hours of the dusk, when I withdraw to a lonesome and

> unfrequented spot, seating myself, leaning my face
> in my hands …
> Hours discouraged, distracted—for the one I cannot
> content myself without, soon I saw him content
> himself without me …
> Sullen and suffering hours! (I am ashamed—but it is
> useless—I am what I am;)
> Hours of my torment—I wonder if other men ever have
> the like, out of the like feelings?
> Is there even one other like me—distracted—his
> friend, his lover, lost to him?

But he was unwilling to publish his pain, perhaps because it would contradict the triumphant proclamation of sexual love in his work, so he removed this poem from the collection, and all that was left of his suffering in the final publication was:

> (I loved a certain person ardently and my love was not
> return'd,
> Yet out of that I have written these songs.)

Fred's letters show that he felt truly bonded to the older man. When Whitman went to Boston to oversee the third edition of *Leaves of Grass*, Fred paid a visit to Whitman's mother and wrote to him several times, declaring his eagerness to see the page proofs of the new book. Judging by his neat penmanship and mostly correct spelling, even though he worked as a deckhand on the Fulton Ferry and a Manhattan coach driver, Fred was probably the most literate of the poet's intimate young companions. After he attended a lecture by Emerson, who had said that men whose hearts were filled with enduring unshakable friendship ought to be set apart from other men and almost worshiped as saints, Fred commented jocularly:

What do you think of them setting you & myself, and one or two others we know up in some public place, with an immense placard on our breast, reading *Sincere Freinds*!!! [sic] Good doctrine that but I think the theory preferable to the practice.

Although their daily contact lasted for little more than a year, until Vaughan moved to other quarters, they continued to stay in touch. It was probably Whitman who cooled down once he accepted the fact that although Fred loved him as a friend, they would not be lifelong lovers. Two years later, Fred got a young woman pregnant and had to marry her. He urged Walt to attend the quiet ceremony:

> Walt,
>   I am to be marri'd tomorrow, Saturday at 3 o'cl[ock] at 213 W. 43rd St.—near 8th Ave.
>   I shall have no show! I have invited no company.—
>   *I want you to be there.—*
>   Do not fail please, as I am very anxious you should come.—
>   Truly yours, Fred

It would not be the only time in Whitman's life that he was invited to the wedding of a young man he had hoped would be his own life partner.

The "Calamus" poems show that Whitman wanted an ideally understanding lover. In "A Glimpse," he describes a tavern scene where he and his ideal mate are in such perfect communion that they barely need to speak, seemingly invisible in their own private dimension right in the midst of a "straight" men's hangout:

Of a crowd of workmen and drivers in a bar-room around
  the stove late of a winter night, and I unremark'd,
  seated in a corner,
Of a youth who loves me and whom I love, silently
  approaching and seating himself near, that he may
  hold me by the hand,
A long while amid the noises of coming and going, of
  drinking and oath and smutty jest,
There we two, content, happy in being together,
  speaking little, perhaps not a word.

Of course, without the social categories of "straight" and "gay" to define opposing camps, the poet might simply regard the men in the bar as friends, but if they had chosen to notice, how would they have regarded two men holding hands like lovers?

In "What Think You I Take My Pen in Hand?" he describes another pair of men showing affection in public:

[T]wo simple men I saw to-day on the pier in the midst
  of the crowd, parting the parting of dear friends,
The one to remain hung on the other's neck and
  passionately kiss'd him
While the one to depart tightly prest the one to
  remain in his arms.

Most of the public chose not to be aware of such displays, but to one who shared similar feelings, they were clearly inspirational.

Abandoning his earlier symbol of the live-oak to represent manly attachment, Whitman selected instead the east coast pond grass called calamus, which has a noticeably large phallic projection. He declared its significance in "These I Singing in Spring":

(O here I last saw him that tenderly loves me, and
 returns again never to separate from me,
And this, O this shall henceforth be the token of
 comrades, this calamus-root shall,
Interchange it youths with each other! let none render
 it back!) ...
I will give of it, but only to them that love as I
 myself am capable of loving.

He invested the plant with a kind of ritual significance, as if
he were summoning together a secret brotherhood. Small
wonder that all over the English-speaking world men who
were attracted to other men imagined they heard a call to
community.

It is generally believed that the "Calamus" section of *Leaves
of Grass* contains Whitman's homoerotic poetry, and that the
"Children of Adam" section contains the heterosexual poetry,
but so many poems were shifted back and forth, with their pronouns altered to accommodate these changes that even a careful
study of the editing process might not reveal the full truth of
the poet's feelings. Some of the most homoerotic poems like
"Native Moments" ended up in the "Children of Adam" section. One theory is that he expressed his true emotions in
"Calamus" and then added "Children of Adam" in order to
create a more universal sexuality, resulting in what would be
called "bisexual" today. A better term might be "pansexual,"
since all of nature is eroticized in Whitman's work. But it
remains clear that his heart is in the poems that deal with his
special brand of comradeship. Borrowing the phrenological
term for male–male love, Whitman declares in "Not Heaving
from My Ribb'd Breast Only": "O adhesiveness! O pulse of my
life!"

Soon after he arrived in Boston, Ralph Waldo Emerson paid

a call. During a two-hour walk on Boston Common, Emerson pleaded with Whitman to remove the "Children of Adam" poems from *Leaves of Grass* on the grounds that their coarsely explicit sexuality might damage the book's sales. He paid no attention to the "Calamus" poems, apparently unable to even imagine that they could be about anything more sexual than simple friendship. Whitman, of course, refused to alter his impassioned verses. On the surface, his decision did not injure the relationship between the two writers, not even if the other famous writers of Boston—Henry Wadsworth Longfellow, James Russell Lowell and Oliver Wendell Holmes—refused to receive him at their club, and not even if the wives of Emerson and Bronson Alcott refused to invite him to their homes. Twelve years later, however, when Emerson published *Parnassus,* an anthology of American verse, Walt Whitman's poetry was not included.

chapter SIX

The Wound Dresser

*Many a soldier's loving arms about this neck have
  cross'd and rested,
Many a soldier's kiss dwells on these bearded lips.*
                              —"The Wound Dresser"

A MOOD OF DREAD HUNG over the country as the 1860s began. The rhetoric had grown angrier and more resolute between the industrial North and the agrarian, slaveholding South, and war was imminent. In 1860 Whitman included a romanticized view of military life in "A Song of Joys":

> O to resume the joys of the soldier!
> To feel the presence of a brave commanding officer—
>   to feel his sympathy!
> To behold his calmness—to be warm'd in the rays of
>   his smile ...

His view of war was innocent then, but although he would continue to find soldiers intensely attractive, it would not be long before his outlook would become less starry-eyed.

On the night of April 13, 1861 Whitman was leaving the opera at a theater on Fourteenth Street, and as he walked down Broadway toward the Brooklyn Ferry he heard shouts in the distance, growing closer. Soon there were newsboys rushing up the street waving copies of a special newspaper edition announcing that Confederate troops had fired on the flag at Fort Sumter. America's greatest national agony had begun.

Ultimately, Whitman would rank the war, along with his parental heritage and his Long Island boyhood, as among the three greatest influences on his life, but it would be another year and a half before he would be drawn more closely into it. His ardor for the preservation of the American union led him at first to adopt a militant posture, calling everyone to arms in "Beat! Beat! Drums!":

> Beat! beat! drums!—Blow! bugles! blow!
> Through the windows—through doors—burst like a
>   ruthless force,

Into the solemn church and scatter the congregation,
Into the school where the scholar is studying;
Leave not the bridegroom quiet—no happiness must he
  have now with his bride,
Nor the peaceful farmer any peace, ploughing his field
  or gathering his grain,
So fierce you pound and whirr you drums—so shrill
  you bugles blow.

Whitman was in his forties and too old to be a soldier, even if he had wanted to, but he was willing to use his writing in support of the Union's cause. Later, when he had seen more of what war does to men, using his "catalogue" (or list) technique in "First O Songs for a Prelude," he would describe the same mobilization he had once so stridently called for with a newer, more wistful tone:

To the drum-taps prompt, the young men falling in and
  arming,
The mechanics arming (the trowel, the jack-plane, the
  blacksmith's hammer, tost aside with precipitation,)
The lawyer leaving his office and arming, the judge
  leaving the court,
The driver deserting his wagon in the street, jumping
  down, throwing the reins abruptly down on the
  horses' backs,
The salesman leaving the store, the boss, book-keeper,
  porter, all leaving;
Squads gathering everywhere by common consent and arm,
The new recruits, even boys ...
(How good they look as they tramp down to the river,
  sweaty, with their guns on their shoulders!
How I love them! how I could hug them, with their

brown faces and their clothes and knapsacks cover'd
with dust!)

The 1860 edition of *Leaves of Grass* was received with mixed
reactions. This time, most of the offended critics were men who
found the book nearly obscene. One of them, a Mr. Beach,
wrote:

> Walt Whitman assumes to regard woman only as an instru-
> ment for the gratification of his desires, and the propagation
> of the species. To him all women are the same, with but this
> difference; the more sensual have the preference, as they
> promise greater indulgence.... with him the congress of the
> sexes is a purely animal affair, and with his ridiculous ego-
> tism he vaunts his prowess as a stock-breeder might that of
> the pick of his herd.

He couldn't have been more wrong, yet he actually ended by
suggesting that the poet commit suicide! Surprisingly, several
women—including Mrs. Beach—rose to defend the book's nat-
uralness and its promise of ultimately being accepted as a new
kind of poetry.

The first examples of the parodies of his work that would
continue until well after his death were published in the *New
York Saturday Press* and *Vanity Fair*. The following one portrays
Whitman as a "counter-jumper," a (frequently effete) salesman
in a dry goods store who might be called a "ribbon clerk" today:

> I am the Counter-jumper, weak and effeminate.
> I love to loaf and lie about dry-goods.
> I loaf and invite the Buyer.
> I am the essence of retail ...
> For I am the creature of weak depravities;

I am the Counter-jumper;
I sound my feeble yelp over the roofs of the World.
(Saunders, 18)

Pained by the ugly criticism, Whitman once again wrote anony-
mous articles defending his own work. His publishers, Thayer and
Eldridge, did their best to promote the book, but their resources
were limited, and the following year they declared bankruptcy.

While the war was still distant, the poet continued selling his
journalism along with an occasional poem and went on about
his usual private life. Perhaps spurred by the urgency of the
war's potential danger, men were led to seize what immediate
pleasures they might. Starting in 1861, the lists in Whitman's
notebooks included more detailed information about some of
his encounters. In a few cases, he wrote that he took men home
"to sleep." Although historians are not certain that the term had
the same sexual connotation that it has in the 21st century, and
although it was customary for men to share beds in rooming
houses and the like, it remains difficult to explain without reference to sex why anyone would take strange men, some of them
neighbors, home to take naps. It is not difficult to construct
various stories based on these entries:

Dec 28 [1861]—Saturday night Mike Ellis—wandering at
the cor of Lexington av. & 32d st.—took him home to 150
37th street,—4th story back room—bitter cold night—
works in Stevenson's Carriage factory./

Dan'l Spencer (Spencer, père, 214 44th st. & 59 William
somewhat feminine—5th av (44) (May 29th)—told me he
had never been in a fight and did not drink at all ... slept
with me Sept. 3rd ...

Theodore M Carr—Deserted Capt. Dawson's Co. C Mon-
itors Co. C Col Conks 139th Reg. N.Y. Vol—met Fort

Greene forenoon Aug. 28—and came to the house with me—is from Greenville Greene County 15 miles from Cox-sackie left Sept. 11th '62.

David Wilson night of Oct. 11 '62 walking up from Mid-dagh—slept with me—works in blacksmith shop in Navy Yard—lives in Hampden st.—walks together Sunday after-noon & night—is about 19—

Horace Ostrander Oct. 22 '62 24 2th av. from Otsego co. 60 miles west of Albany was in the hospital to see Chas. Green) about 28 y'rs of age ... slept with him Dec. 4th '62 ...

Jerry Taylor, (NJ.) of 2d dist reg't slept with me last night weather soft, cool enough, warm enough, heavenly

He also continued his earlier habit of riding and talking with the stage drivers up and down Broadway, and when they were ill he visited them in the hospital, which turned out to be good practice for the duties he would undertake during the war.

Whitman's brother George had enlisted in the army and was wounded in the fighting near Fredericksburg, Virginia. In December 1862, it fell to Walt to try to find him. After searching through the hospitals in Washington, Walt traveled to the site of the battle and was shocked by what he found there. Outside the field hospital at the base of a tree, he stumbled upon a large pile of amputated hands, arms, feet, and legs. Given the lack of modern surgical techniques and medications, amputation was the most common means of dealing with wounds to the limbs during the Civil War. Several dead bodies lay alongside the mound of limbs, and at that moment he real-ized the truth of the war.

Luckily his brother had not been seriously wounded and was already back in action, so Walt turned his attention to the other wounded men, who captured his heart with their beauty and their suffering. In the same hospital, he met a 19-year-old

Confederate captain from Mississippi and wrote to his friends at home that "our affection is quite romantic." From the start, it made no difference to him whether the wounded soldiers were from the North or the South. They were simply handsome young American men, and they needed him. He stayed with his brother for a while, getting to know the men in the camps and gathering material to write about, but he decided that the place where he could play his part was in the hospitals.

At the end of 1862, he returned to Washington, where he encountered William Douglas O'Connor, a novelist and abolitionist whom he had met on his trip to Boston. Both O'Connor and his wife Ellen (called Nellie) took a fancy to the earnest poet, and soon he was established in a room in the house where they rented an apartment and shared their meals with him. He found a job as a copyist in the army paymaster's office to support himself, and he devoted his free time to visiting the boys in the hospitals. During the course of the war, he described some of them in his diaries:

> Janus Mayfield (bed 59 Ward 6 Camp[bell] Hosp.) about 18 years old, 7th Virginia Vol. Has three brothers also in the Union Army. Illiterate, but cute—can neither read nor write. Has been very sick and low, but now recovering. have visited him regularly for two weeks, given him money, fruit, candy, &c.
>
> Ward G Armory May 12 William Williams co F. 27th Indiana/ wounded seriously in shoulder—he lay naked to the waist on acc't of the heat—I never saw a more superb development of chest, & limbs, neck &c a perfect model of manly strength—seemed awful to take such God's masterpiece ...
>
> Albion F Hubbard—Ward C bed 7 Co F 1st Mass Cavalry/been in the service one year—has had two carbuncles

one on arm, one in ankle, healing at present yet great holes
left, stuffed with rags—worked on a farm 8 years before
enlisting—wrote letter—for him to the man he lived
with/died June 20th '63

Ward K Armory Sq Hosp ... a young Ohio boy, Oscar
Cunningham badly wounded in right leg—his history is a sad
one—he has been here nearly a year—He & I have been quite
intimate all that time. When he was brought here I thought he
ought to have been taken by a sculptor to model for an
emblematical figure of the west, he was such a handsome
young giant, over 6 feet high, a great head of brown yellowy
shining hair thick & longish & manly noble manner & talk—
he has suffered very much, since the doctors have been trying
to save his leg but it will probably have to be taken off yet. He
wants it done, but I think [he] is too weak at present.

Modeling himself after a woman he had seen tending to the
soldiers who had been taken to the hospital in New York where
he had visited the ailing stage drivers, Whitman took it upon
himself to bring gifts of oranges, apples, candy, and tobacco to
the boys; writing letters home for those who were unschooled
or too ill to hold a pen; holding their hands and telling them
stories; and offering them what comfort he could. Whitman's
compassion may have been motivated, at least in part, by his
attraction to these handsome young men. Some critics have
suggested that his sexual desire for these young men was easily
satisfied by them, but that is debatable. Surely he wanted them,
but it is not clear that they understood that. Probably very few
of them were open to sexual encounters with other men, but
most of them, lonely and injured and far from home, were
open to the parental nurture he offered them and were grateful
for his kind attentions, including his kisses and caresses.

In more than one case he fell deeply in love with them and

fantasized a life with them once the war was over. Lewis Kirk Brown, who enlisted at the age of 18, and whom Whitman called Lewy, was one of the foremost among them. He had received a serious wound to the leg, and when Whitman was unable to visit him, he wrote to the young man in the hospital, saying the sight of Lewy's face was "welcomer than all" and calling him "my darling" and "my dear son & comrade." Like most of Whitman's young wards, Lewy was embarrassed about his lack of literary skills when writing to his eloquent mentor, but Whitman assured him:

> —you say I must excuse you for writing so much foolish-ness—nothing of the kind—my darling boy when you write to me, you must write without ceremony. I like to hear every little thing about yourself & your affairs,—you need never care how you write to me Lewy, if you will only—I never think about literary perfection in letters either, it is the man & the feeling—

Whitman went so far as to share with Lewy his fantasy of their future:

> O Lewy how glad I should be to see you, to have you with me—I have thought if it could be so that you & one other person & myself could be where we could work & live together, & have each other's society, we three, I should like it so much—but it is probably a dream ...

Whitman's dedication to Lewy was real. After many months of hospitalization, it was determined that his left leg could not be saved and had to be amputated five inches below the knee. Whitman was present at the surgery and stayed in a cot next to Lewy's bed for two nights while he recovered.

As honest as his feelings were, Whitman's suggestion of "one other person" was significant. Looking at all of the major relationships of his life from this point on, we can see that there was something that kept his affections from being totally exclusive. During each relationship there is at least the hint of his covert attraction, and perhaps dalliance, with some other man. It likely was his ability to find beauty in all men that lent this touch of promiscuity to his affections, even if he wasn't always able to act them out. At the same time that he was so dedicated to Lewy Brown, he was even more passionately attracted to Lewy's friend, Sergeant Thomas P. Sawyer, called Tom. Whitman's letters to Tom openly mentioned his affection for Lewy:

> Lew is so good, so affectionate—when I came away he reached up his face [and] I put my arm around him and we gave each other a long kiss half a minute long.

It might have been unseemly for such a lengthy kiss to take place in a crowded ward where so many other patients could see the two men, but there was a Ward Master's room where some privacy was available. Wherever it took place, its duration was probably encouraged more by Whitman's ardor than by the weakened Lewy's ability to clasp the poet to him, no matter how grateful he was. Perhaps Whitman's reason for describing Lewy's kiss in detail was to hint to Tom what was hoped for from him. His suggestion to Lewy about living with one other person after the war was clearly part of a plan he had envisioned about Tom and had mentioned to him as well:

> Dear comrade, you must not forget me, for I never shall you. My love you have in life or death, forever. I don't know how you feel about it, but it is the wish of my heart to have your

friendship and also that if you should come safe out of this war, we should come together again in some place where we could make our living, and be true comrades and never be separated while life lasts—and take Lew Brown too, and never separate from him. Or if things are not so to be—if you get these lines, my dear darling comrade, and any thing should go wrong, so that we do not meet again, here on earth, it seems to me (the way I feel now), that my soul could never entirely be happy, even in the world to come, without you, dear Comrade.

Sawyer probably was taken aback by the urgency and inappropriateness of the poet's feelings and perhaps did not know what to make of this man who was nearly twice his age. Although Whitman bought him a shirt and a pair of drawers, he neglected to pick them up before leaving for the military camp, and the poet's feelings were hurt. Whitman wrote to him:

> [I]t would have been a satisfaction to me if you had accepted them. I should have often thought now Tom may be wearing around his body something from me ... Now my dearest comrade, I will bid you so long, & hope God will put it in your heart to bear toward me a little at least of the feeling I have about you. If it is only a quarter as much I shall be satisfied ...

Sawyer wrote his apology, explaining in his barely literate spelling that he was in such a rush that he had forgotten to pick up the gifts. He dutifully called Whitman "Dear Brother," but it was clear that his passions were nothing like Whitman's, and although he wrote to the poet again, there was ultimately no ongoing relationship between Whitman and Lewy and Tom. Sergeant Sawyer did promise to keep "for old acquantance [sic]

Sake" the little book he had been given, which was more than likely a copy of *Leaves of Grass*.

In November 1863, Whitman traveled to New York to visit with his beloved mother, to whom he had written frequently during his year away from home. There he found his brother Andrew in the advanced stages of alcoholism, draining his mother's resources while his brother Jesse was beginning to act more and more strangely, barely able to contain his rage. Whitman hated to leave his mother in such circumstances, even if his brother Jeff was there to help, but the wounded and dying men in Washington had become his first priority. Shortly after his return to the capital, he learned that Andrew had died, but he did not go back to Brooklyn for the funeral.

Whitman not only visited the hospitals, he also went to the battle sites to get a first-hand view, and he kept notes on what he saw. Although he claimed that "the real war will never get in the books," he later published his descriptions of the war years along with entries on many other subjects from his journal

The Civil War by the Numbers

In terms of casualties, the Civil War remains the bloodiest war in American history. More than three million men fought in the Civil War, and more than 620,000 men died. Disease claimed twice as many victims as battle wounds did. The Battle of Antietam proved to be the bloodiest day of the war with over 22,000 casualties—by comparison, Allied casualties on D-Day numbered over 9,000. The principle weapon of the war was a single-shot, muzzle loading rifle that had a maximum range of about 1000 yards and could be loaded at a rate of three times a minute. Many of the doctors who served in the civil war had never been to medical school, and though he had no official training, Walt Whitman often acted as a male nurse to the soldiers.

under the title *Specimen Days*, a book which became the most
accurate written documentation of the scenes of the war and its
aftermath, a verbal equivalent to the magnificent photographs
of Matthew Brady. Shortly after the battle of Chancellorsville,
he went to the battlefield and described the horrible carnage
that he found there, a stunning contrast to the serenity of
nature:

> The night was very pleasant, at times the moon shining out
> full and clear, all Nature so calm in itself, the early summer
> grass so rich, and foliage of the trees—yet there the battle
> raging and many good fellows lying helpless ... amid the
> rattle of muskets and crash of cannon ... the red life-blood
> oozing out from heads or trunks or limbs upon the green
> and dew-cool grass. Patches of the woods take fire, and sev-
> eral of the wounded, unable to move, are consumed—quite
> large spaces are swept over, burning the dead also—some of
> the men have their hair and beards singed—some, burns on
> their faces and hands—others holes burnt in their clothing
> ... we hear the secesh [i.e., the secessionist Southerners]
> yells—our men cheer loudly back ... hand to hand conflicts,
> each side stands up to it, brave, determin'd as demons, they
> often charge upon us ...
>
> Then the camps of the wounded—O heavens, what scene
> is this?—is this indeed humanity—these butchers' shambles?
> There are several of them. There they lie, in the largest, in an
> open space in the woods, from 200 to 300 poor fellows—the
> groans and screams—the odor of blood, mixed with the
> fresh scent of the night, the grass, the trees—that slaughter-
> house! O well is it their mothers, their sisters cannot see
> them—cannot conceive, and never conceiv'd, these things.
> One man is shot by a shell, both in the arm and leg—both
> are amputated—there lie the rejected members. Some have

their legs blown off—some bullets through the breast—some indescribably horrid wounds in the face or head, all mutilated, sickening, torn, gouged out—some in the abdomen—some mere boys—many rebels, badly hurt—they take their regular turns with the rest, just the same as any—the surgeons use them just the same ... while over all the clear, large moon comes out at times softly, quietly shining. Amid the woods, that scene of flitting souls—amid the crack and crash and yelling sounds—the impalpable perfume of the woods—and yet the pungent, stifling smoke—the radiance of the moon ...

Whitman's experiences in the war, both real and imagined, also became the source of a section of *Leaves of Grass* called "Drum Taps," with poems ranging from the calls to arms cited above to portraits of the troops at war—marching, crossing rivers, camping in tents—to the story of an elderly farm couple receiving the news that their son has been killed. One of the tenderest of the war poems is "Vigil Strange I Kept on the Field One Night," in which he returns after the battle to sit up with the body of a dead soldier, whom he calls in the words he used for the men he loved, "my son and comrade":

Found you in death so cold dear comrade, found your
  body son of responding kisses (never again on earth
  responding,) ...
But not a tear fell, not even a long-drawn sigh, long,
  long I gazed,
Then on the earth partially reclining sat by your side
  leaning my chin in my hands,
Passing sweet hours, immortal and mystic hours with
  you dearest comrade—not a tear, not a word ...
I faithfully loved you and cared for you living, I

think we shall surely meet again ...
I rose from the chill ground and folded my soldier
  well in his blanket,
And buried him where he fell.

The long hours he spent in hospital wards and visiting the army bivouacs were wearing on the poet, and in his own way he began to be a victim of the war like so many others. In spite of his robust appearance, his health was beginning to deteriorate, and he was less energetic than he had been, but he kept up his work as diligently as before, and surrounded by so many people who were making sacrifices greater than his, the man who had once liked to consider himself a loafer now drove himself harder than ever.

chapter
seven

The Tenderest Lover

Publish my name and hang up my picture as that of the
* tenderest lover,*
The friend the lover's portrait, of whom his friend
* his lover was fondest,*
Who was not proud of his songs, but of the measureless
* ocean of love within him, and freely pour'd it forth ...*
—"Recorders Ages Hence"

AS WHITMAN WALKED THE STREETS of Washington during the war years, he occasionally encountered the tall, angular, black-clad figure of Abraham Lincoln, who nodded a greeting to him. Whitman admired the president, almost to the point of idolizing him. He wrote in his journal:

(I never see that man without feeling that he is one to become personally attached to, for his combination of purest, heartiest tenderness, and native western form of manliness.)

Describing the president in a letter to friends, he said:

I think well of the President. He has a face like a hoosier Michael Angelo, so awful ugly it becomes beautiful, with its strange mouth, its deep cut, criss-cross lines, and its doughnut complexion.

The poet could see the travails of war written on the commander-in-chief's face and sympathized with him, writing in a letter to his mother:

He looks more careworn even than usual—his face with deep cut lines, seams, & his *complexion gray*, through very dark skin, a curious looking man, very sad—I said to a lady who was looking with me, "Who can see that man without losing all wish to be sharp upon him personally? Who can say he has not a good soul?"

Whitman was making new friends in the capital. Aside from William and Nellie O'Connor, he met John T. Trowbridge, a writer of biography, and John Burroughs, a nature writer, who had a job as a clerk in the Treasury Department. Burroughs was charmed by Whitman, whom he described in a letter as looking "glorious" and "like a god." In another letter, he said, "He loves everything and everybody. I saw a soldier the other day stop on the street and kiss him. He kisses me as if I were a girl." (Myerson, 313) Despite this description, there is no indication that there was anything sexual between Whitman and Burroughs. Their relationship was based on the things they had in common, a love of nature and literature. Whitman had developed two mutually exclusive circles of friends to meet his different needs. The young soldiers, who were often illiterate farmboys and laborers, must have reminded him of the omnibus drivers and boat pilots he had enjoyed back in New York; the writers and literary people, who could understand and appreciate his poetry, provided him with stimulating conversation. In the manner of other literary men attracted to working-class men, he traveled comfortably in both worlds as a full citizen of each.

Whitman's war experience did not turn him against the men of the South. Rather, he rose above the nation's political divisions, remaining aware of the humanity of all concerned, as in his poem "Reconciliation":

> For my enemy is dead, a man divine as myself is dead,
> I look where he lies white-faced and still in the
>   coffin—I draw near,
> Bend down and touch lightly with my lips the white
>   face in the coffin.

His work in the hospitals became increasingly depressing, with more and more cases of diarrhea to tend to, as well as greater numbers of soldiers driven mad by their battlefield experiences. The ward personnel were not always sympathetic to the patients, but Whitman continued to do his best, taking on distasteful tasks, even though he himself was beginning to suffer dizzy spells, headaches, and sore throats. In the middle of 1864, he returned to his mother's house to recuperate, and he stayed for the remainder of the year, resuming his writing even though he never fully recovered from his symptoms. At the end of the year, he had the sad task of committing his brother Jesse, who had grown increasingly violent, to an asylum. Shortly thereafter came the news that his brother George had been captured in battle and was being held in a Confederate prisoner of war camp. Finally, at the beginning of 1865, Whitman was offered a job in the Department of the Interior as a clerk at the Bureau of Indian Affairs, and he decided to return to Washington.

Since he followed his usual custom of arriving at the office late and leaving early, his job left him time to continue his writing, his visits to the hospitals, and his efforts to secure George's release. He attended Lincoln's second inaugural celebration, and soon after things began to look up. George was finally part of a prisoner exchange. Whitman took a leave of absence from his job and went to Brooklyn to visit his returning brother, whom he found emaciated from the starvation rations he had been fed in the camp, but alive and well.

At last, early in April, General Lee surrendered to General Grant at Appomattox, and within days the war was over. Whitman spent some time arranging for the printing of his wartime poems, *Drum-Taps*, and looking forward to a happy Easter dinner, when suddenly the breath was knocked out of him. On April 14, while watching the play *Our American Cousin* at Ford's Theater in Washington, his beloved Abraham Lincoln was assassinated. The Whitman family heard the news the following morning. Unable to eat, Whitman wandered up Broadway in the rain, looking at the silent shuttered storefronts draped in black and joining the crowds in front of the newspaper offices. His holiday was over. At the beginning of the week, he returned to Washington.

He watched the staid funeral procession pass through the streets of Washington and later watched the funeral train leave on its mournful journey back to Springfield, Illinois. He immediately wrote a short poem to commemorate the occasion, "Hush'd Be the Camps To-Day." Soon afterward, he wrote one of his least artistic poems, "Oh Captain! My Captain!", which uses a sing-song rhythm, a rigid rhyme scheme, and mawkish imagery to honor the fallen leader. In spite of—or perhaps because of—its reversion to a style he had already superseded, it became a beloved standard in elementary schools throughout the nation:

> O Captain! my Captain! our fearful trip is done,
> The ship has weather'd every rack, the prize we sought
>   is won,
> The port is near, the bells I hear, the people all
>   exulting,
> While follow eyes, the steady keel, the vessel grim
>   and daring;
>   But O heart! heart! heart!
>   O the bleeding drops of red,
>   Where on the deck my Captain lies,
>   Fallen cold and dead.

Not long afterwards, he was able to compose one of his most beautiful poems, "When Lilacs Last in the Dooryard Bloom'd," using the traditional poetic form of the elegy to express his grief in majestically phrased verses and symbols—the lilacs which represent his love and the star which represents Lincoln:

> When lilacs last in the dooryard bloom'd,

And the great star early droop'd in the western sky in
  the night,
I mourn'd, and yet shall mourn with ever-returning
  spring.

He describes the passage of Lincoln's funeral train through a
stunned America:

Coffin that passes through lanes and streets ...
With the pomp of the inloop'd flags with the cities
  draped in black,
With the show of the States themselves as of crape-
  veiled women standing ...
With the countless torches lit, with the silent sea of
  faces and the unbared heads ...
With dirges through the night, with the thousand
  voices rising strong and solemn ...
With the tolling tolling bells' perpetual clang,
Here, coffin that slowly passes,
I give you my sprig of lilac ...
O death, I cover you over with roses and early lilies ...

The song of a thrush is used to represent the poet's sorrow:

O singer bashful and tender, I hear your notes, I hear
  your call,
I hear, I come presently, I understand you ...
And how shall I deck my song for the large sweet soul
  that has gone?
And what shall my perfume be for the grave of him I
  love? ...

Finally, he takes his leave of Lincoln, calling him "the sweetest wisest soul of all my days and lands." For the remainder of his life, Whitman commemorated President Lincoln's death annually, almost as a religious obligation.

In May 1865, Whitman finally published the *Drum-Taps* poems he had been composing during the war. They were his tribute to the countless fallen soldiers and his dedication to love as the source of the republic's strength rather than war, which had become too painfully real for him. One poem, "Over the Carnage Rose Prophetic a Voice," written before the war, was eventually made part of *Drum-Taps* because it expressed this message so clearly:

> Be not dishearten'd, affection shall solve the
> problems of freedom yet,
> Those who love each other shall become invincible ...

Lincoln's Assassination

On the night of April 14, 1865, while attending a special performance of "Our American Cousin" at Ford's Theater, John Wilkes Booth entered the presidential box and fired his derringer pistol, killing President Lincoln. The bullet entered through Lincoln's left ear and logged behind his right eye. Lincoln was paralyzed and carried across the street to a boarding house where he died the next morning at 7:22 AM. Lincoln's body lay in state in the newly constructed Rotunda of the U.S. Capitol from April 19 to April 21 before making it's way back to Illinois. Along the way, funeral processions were held in numerous cities including Philadelphia, New York City, Cleveland, and Chicago. Whitman, always impressed by Lincoln, penned his now famous poem "O Captain! My Captain!" in response to Lincoln's assassination.

It shall be customary in the houses and streets to see
  manly affection,
The most dauntless and rude shall touch face to face
  lightly,
The dependence of Liberty shall be lovers,
The continuance of Equality shall be comrades.

Here we can see the several most important strands of Whitman's thought woven together. His homoerotic feelings are bound up in his spiritual sensibility, and together they create the loving comradeship that is at the base of his patriotic affirmation of democracy. In spite of his good intentions, however, his poetry was still regarded as immoral by some. In June, when James Harlan, a former Methodist minister, became the new Secretary of the Interior and therefore Whitman's new boss, he asked for reports on the loyalty and moral character of the staff. Whitman had been working on a manuscript of *Leaves of Grass* in preparation for a new edition, and when a copy of it was discovered in his desk, he was summarily fired.

With the help of his friends, Whitman was without much difficulty able to get another job, this one in the Attorney General's office, but his admirers remained outraged by his dismissal. Probably with considerable assistance from Whitman, William Douglas O'Connor wrote a pamphlet in defense of him called *The Good Gray Poet*. The title referred to the poet's habit of dressing in a simple Quaker gray suit, suggesting his admirable simplicity and purity. In a discussion of the need for freedom for writers of literature, the pamphlet extolled Whitman as a modern equivalent of Shakespeare, Homer, or Dante, innocent of any charges of immorality and deserving of the nation's gratitude and respect. Even if O'Connor's defense was somewhat overenthusiastic, the nickname of "Good Gray Poet" stuck.

Despite O'Connor's aggrandizement of Whitman, *Drum-Taps* and the slim sequel to it that Whitman produced soon afterward were not very well received. One of the most stringent critics of Whitman and his work was the young author Henry James. For him, Whitman's sympathy with the soldiers of the Civil War was not enough to make him the poet of America:

> To become adopted as a national poet, it is not enough to ... amass crudity upon crudity, to discharge the undigested contents of your blotting-book into the lap of the public. You must respect the public which you address; for it has taste, if you have not. (Allen, 360)

A mere glance through the poet's painstakingly revised manuscripts will show that James's accusation that his work was "undigested" was totally wrong. Putting such undeserved criticism aside, Whitman continued working at his job, visiting the soldiers who still remained in the hospitals, and spending time with his literary friends. In December 1865, he was on his way home from such a visit when he met Peter Doyle, an 18-year-old veteran of the Confederate army, now working as a horse-car conductor, who was to become one of the great loves of Whitman's life. Doyle had Irish good looks, with a small mustache, a rounded nose, and a twinkle in his eye. In an interview several decades later, Doyle described their first encounter on a stormy night:

> Walt had his blanket—it was thrown round his shoulders—he seemed like an old sea-captain. He was the only passenger, it was a lonely night, so I thought I would go in and talk with him. Something in me made me do it and something in him drew me that way. He used to say there

was something in me had the same effect on him. Anyway, I went into the car. We were familiar at once—I put my hand on his knee—we understood. He did not get out at the end of the trip—in fact went all the way back with me ... From that time on we were the biggest sort of friends.

Whitman and Doyle became daily companions, bringing flowers to one another, taking long walks along the Potomac, visiting Pete's family in Alexandria, Virginia, and later visiting Walt's family in New York. Pete had been at Ford's Theater on the night of Lincoln's assassination, and he gave Whitman a first-hand account of the shocked audience's reactions. But it was Whitman who was the teacher, as he had been with Fred Vaughan half a dozen years earlier. Whitman was 46 when they met, two and a half times Pete's age, and he was well read, while Pete was practically illiterate. During their walks, Walt talked to his young friend about everything from astronomy to religion to poetry to politics. Pete enthusiastically drank in this education, grateful for the attention of this wise and worldly man.

Sometimes they were like boys together. When they bought a fresh watermelon and sat on the curb to cut it open, more refined people laughed at them, and Pete felt embarrassed. "Let them have the laughs," Whitman told him. "We've got the watermelon!" They posed for photographs together, staring lovingly into one another's eyes. At last a great gap in Whitman's life was filled. He had the dedicated companion he had long dreamed of.

His ideal companion took many forms, not just that of a friend and comrade. During 1866, Whitman worked on a new edition of *Leaves of Grass*, including a thoroughly revised version of his earlier poem "Proto-Leaf," now retitled "Starting from Paumanok." In it, he addresses a figure he calls his "camerado," who appears in several other of his poems, for example in "Song of Myself," as "the great *Camerado*, the lover true for whom I pine." The term is an Old English form of the Spanish word *camarada*, which Whitman found in his youthful reading of Sir Walter Scott's *Waverly Novels*. For Whitman it meant his ideal mate: partly God, partly lover, partly friend, partly son, partly mentor and partly muse:

> What do you need camerado?
> Dear son do you think it is love? ...
> It is a painful thing to love a man or woman to
>   excess, and yet it satisfies, it is great ...

The poem announces the themes of Whitman's poetry: the equality of body and soul, the acceptance of death, the significance of loving comrades, the love of America. It ends with an invocation to the camerado, entwining the spiritual and emotional nature of his bond:

> O camerado close! O you and me at last, and us two
>   only ...
> O something ecstatic and undemonstrable! O music wild!
> O now I triumph—and you shall also;
> O hand in hand—O wholesome pleasure—O one more
>   desirer and lover! ...

Of course, Peter Doyle could not fulfill all the functions of Whitman's ideal camerado. One of his failings may have been that he couldn't fully comprehend Whitman's writing. Nonetheless, he became Whitman's daily companion for the next seven years, and he remained the poet's lifelong friend.

Although he sought male comradeship as his most intimate form of love, in "Starting from Paumanok," Walt described himself as a manly man, not a sweet person with feminine affectations:

No dainty dolce affettuoso I,
Bearded, sun-burnt, gray-neck'd, forbidding, I have
    arrived,
To be wrestled with as I pass ...

This self-portrait is reinforced in other poems, where he refers to himself as a rugged individual: "Stout as a horse, affectionate, haughty, electrical, I and this mystery here we stand." With carnivorous toughness, he declares: "Hankering, gross, mystical, nude, how is it I extract strength from the beef I eat?" Although his manner was not particularly effeminate, according to those who described him, it was also not as hypermasculine as these self-descriptions would imply. In them, he was on one level creating the fictional persona of "Walt Whitman," his own work of art. On another level, he was drawing a portrait of the natural manly lover of men in his idealized notion of comradeship, an image that society ignored in favor of the effeminate stereotype of the sophisticated urban homosexual for well over a century.

The fourth edition of *Leaves of Grass* appeared in 1867 with no frontispiece image of the author. Whitman did everything he could to promote it, including helping his friend John Burroughs to write a book about him, called *Notes on Walt Whitman as Poet and Person*. This time the reviews were more positive, and most important, the book's reputation became international. William Rossetti, an English critic, wrote an article praising Whitman's poetry, and by the next year, 1868, although the entire *Leaves of Grass* was not published there, an English edition of selected *Poems of Walt Whitman* did appear with an introduction signed by William Douglas O'Connor but actually written by Whitman himself. Despite his efforts to liberate American literature from the influence of European writers, his work was more readily appreciated in Great Britain than it had been in the United States, perhaps because it had been expurgated. Meanwhile, he began to publish individual poems and essays on such subjects as democracy and "personalism" (a doctrine of community based on the transcendental theory of the Oversoul).

Whitman stayed in frequent touch with his mother in Brooklyn. Her semiliterate letters were full of complaints about the tribulations of living with her children. Whitman was clearly her friend and confidant as well as her son, and she was closer to him than to her other children. At first Whitman's favorite brother Jeff and his wife Martha lived with her, but Jeff eventually was appointed Superintendent of Water Works in St. Louis, Missouri, and he moved his family there, leaving Whitman's mother to live with his brother George, who, having recovered from his Civil War experiences, had opened a carpentry shop. When George decided to move his work to Camden, New Jersey, Whitman's mother had little choice but to go with him and his wife Louisa, even though she wasn't very happy about the situation since she was still concerned about her mentally handicapped son Eddy. She hesitated to rely on George since she found him somewhat stingy, and, worse, she was no longer the mistress of her own home.

Through Pete, Whitman became friendly with a circle of horse car drivers and railroad men, whose company he continued to enjoy. One of them, Jim Sorrell, apparently as a joke, sent Whitman a message via Pete saying "the most thing he don't understand is that young Lady that said you make such a good bed fellow." Whether this implies that Sorrell knew—or even had experienced—the truth about Whitman's preferences in bedmates cannot be ascertained, but it is doubtful that it refers to any sexual experience Whitman had with a woman. In a note to Pete, Whitman included a message in response to Sorrell:

Dear Jimmy: You may not understand it, what that lady said about the bedfellow business, but it's all right & regular—besides, I guess you understand it well enough. Jimmy, dear boy, I wish you was here with me—we could have such good times.

None of Whitman's close relationships with men remained exclusive. While he was involved with Peter Doyle, he also met a young streetcar driver named Jack Flood on a trip to New York. When Flood wrote to him, Whitman responded with an invitation to visit him in Washington:

You speak of coming here and paying me a visit. Dear boy, I hope you will come truly, for it would be a great comfort to me if we could be together again. I don't know whether it would be very pleasant to you here, Jack, for this is a stupid place compared to New York—but we would have each other's society, and that would be first rate.... Dear Jack, I send you my love.

Their correspondence continued for several years, at which time Whitman wrote to him, using his nickname, "Johnny":

Johnny, you say you should like to see me—Well, no more than I should to see you, my darling boy. I wish we were together this minute, & you had employment so we could remain with each other, if you would feel satisfied to be so.

Whitman continued to feel unwell from time to time, experiencing dizzy spells and persistent colds and bouts of exhaustion. Pete, too, had a medical condition, a rash on his face that the doctor minimized as a "barber's itch," but which Pete guiltily feared was untreatable syphilis that would prove fatal. He was so worried about it that he actually considered suicide, a prospect that deeply disturbed Whitman, who wrote to Pete during one of his trips:

> How is it with you, dearest boy—and is there anything different with the face? Dear Pete, you must forgive me for being so cold the last day & evening. I was unspeakably shocked and repelled from you by that talk & proposition of yours—you know what—there by the fountain. It seemed indeed to me, (for I will talk out plain to you, dearest comrade) that the one I loved, and who had always been so manly & sensible, was gone, & a fool & intentional murderer stood in his place....
>
> Dearest boy, I have not a doubt but you will get well ... The extreme cases of that malady, (as I told you before) are persons that have very deeply diseased blood, probably with syphilis in it, inherited from parentage ... You are of healthy stock, with a sound constitution & good blood ... My darling, if you are not well when I come back I will get a good room or two in some quiet place ... and we will live together, & devote ourselves altogether to the job of curing you ... I have had this in my mind before, but never broached it to you.
>
> Dear comrade, I think of you very often. My love for you is indestructible, & since that night & morning has returned more than before.
>
> Dear Pete, dear son, my darling boy, my young & loving brother, don't let the devil put such thoughts in your mind again ...

To the life-affirming Whitman, any thought of self-destruction was horrible. His maternal solution to Pete's problem is reminiscent of his devotion to Lewy Brown during the war. Some of Whitman's letters to Pete ended in effusive expressions of love, such as calling him "baby" and this closure to a letter cheering Pete up when he was depressed:

[A]ll I have to say is—to say nothing—only a good smacking kiss, and many of them—& taking in return many, many, many, from my dear son—good loving ones, too—which will do more credit to his lips than growling & complaining at his father.

Despite the language of love and the references to kissing, it remains impossible to determine what, if any, sexual contact there was between Doyle and Whitman. All the information available is consistent with several possible interpretations, but it is clear that their relationship was passionately intense on both sides. The most perplexing evidence is an anguished entry from Whitman's diary of July 15, 1870. He was probably still grieving for the death of his brother Jesse several months earlier, but he turned his attention to his anxiety about his relationship with Pete:

cheating childish abandonment of myself, fancying what does not really exist in another, but is all the time in *myself* alone—utterly deluded and cheated by myself, & my own weakness—REMEMBER WHERE I AM MOST WEAK, & most lacking. Yet always preserve a kind spirit & demeanor to 16. But PURSUE HER NO MORE ... It is IMPERATIVE, that I obviate & remove myself (& my orbit) *at all hazards* from this *incessant enormous* & PERTURBATION ... TO GIVE UP ABSOLUTELY & for good, *from this present hour*, this

FEVERISH, FLUCTUATING, *useless undignified pursuit of 164—too long, (much too long)* persevered in,—so humiliating—*It must come at last* & had better come now—(*It cannot possibly be a success*) LET THERE FROM THIS HOUR BE NO FALTERING, NO GETTING — — *at all henceforth,* (NOT ONCE, under any circumstances) — — *avoid seeing her, or meeting her, or any talk or explanations* — — or ANY MEETING WHATEVER, FROM THIS HOUR FORTH, FOR LIFE.... Depress the adhesive nature / It is in excess—making life a torment / All this diseased, feverish disproportionate *adhesiveness.*

His emotional state caused some of his language to be incoherent, but he was not too upset to attempt to hide what he was talking about. Scholars have determined that "164" is a code, using numerical values for each letter of the alphabet, so that "16" stands for "P" and "4" stands for "D"—Peter Doyle's initials. Also, where the word "her" appears, it is clear that there is an erasure, and that the word "him" originally appeared there. "Adhesiveness," the phrenological term Whitman had borrowed to refer to male–male friendship was easily extended to include homoerotic feelings.

Whitman may have been saying that his sexual feelings in his relationship with Doyle were one-sided, that as close as they had become, they had never been physically intimate—or perhaps they had been intimate early on, but Pete did not wish the relationship to continue on a physical basis. His words sound like those of someone who is afraid to overstep certain boundaries for fear of being rejected. They are full of angry frustration and a self-loathing that is completely inconsistent with the message of self-approval that his poetry had been purveying. Evidently he had interpreted some statement of Pete's to indicate that there was no counterpart to his feelings, but in the following note, written to Pete two weeks after the diary entry, he acknowledged that he had overreacted and that their love—sexual or not—was indeed mutual:

> Dear Pete ... We parted there, you know, at the corner of 7th St., Tuesday night. Pete, there was something in that hour from 10 to 11 o'clock (parting though it was) that has left me pleasure and comfort for good—I never dreamed that you made so much of having me with you, nor that you could feel so downcast at losing me. I foolishly thought it was all on the other side. But all I will say further on the subject is, I now see clearly, that was all wrong.

Whitman added a note to his dramatic diary entry of July 15, drawing on his earlier study of the philosophy of stoicism to outline his concept of a calm character: "[H]is emotions &c are complete in himself irrespective (indifferent) of whether his love, friendship &c are returned or not."

With his relationship intact, Whitman set about preparing the fifth edition of *Leaves of Grass*, which was printed in 1871. Many poems were moved around, and the physical book itself was an improvement over the earlier editions. One new work, "Passage to India" was published in a small volume with selected poems culled from *Leaves of Grass*. It is a description of the technological communication and transportation marvels that were linking the world, symbolizing the spiritual unity of the planet. Ultimately the passage to India comes to represent the passage of the soul to the source of all knowledge, the unknown land beyond life where the answers to all our eternal questions wait:

> Passage to more than India!
> O secret of the earth and sky! ...

Passage, immediate passage! the blood burns in my
  veins!
Away O soul! hoist instantly the anchor! ...
Have we not stood here like trees in the ground long
  enough? ...
Have we not darken'd and dazed ourselves with books
  long enough? ...
O farther, farther, farther sail!

In the same year, "Democratic Vistas," one of Whitman's most important essays was published. He had been writing it in separate sections since 1867. Essentially, it is a criticism of America's flaws by one who loves her. Calling for a new aesthetics to replace the outmoded religious ethics inherited from Europe, he declares that the poet will be the new spiritual leader: "The priest departs, the divine literatus comes." Following the corrosive Civil War, he saw a corruption of national values, a loss of national faith, which he hoped to restore. He angrily took urban Americans to task for surrendering to the pleasures of materialism and failing to live up to the highest ideals of healthy vigor and spirit:

Are there, indeed, men here worthy the name? Are there athletes? Are there perfect women to match the generous material luxuriance? Is there a pervading atmosphere of beautiful manners? Are there crops of fine youths, and majestic old persons? Are there arts worthy freedom and a rich people? Is there a great moral and religious civilization—the only justification of a great material one? ... Confess that everywhere, in shop, street, church, theatre, barroom, official chair, are pervading flippancy and vulgarity, low cunning, infidelity—everywhere the youth puny, impudent, foppish, prematurely ripe—everywhere an abnormal libidinousness, unhealthy forms, male, female, painted, padded, dyed, chignon'd, muddy complexions, bad blood, the capacity for good motherhood deceasing or deceas'd, shallow notions of beauty, with a range of manners, or rather lack of manners (considering the advantages enjoy'd), probably the meanest to be seen in the world.

The way to heal the problem of society at large, he believed, was to create the finest kind of individuals:

> To our model, a clear-blooded, strong-fibered physique is indispensable; the questions of food, drink, air, exercise, assimilation, digestion, can never be intermitted. Out of these we descry a well-begotten selfhood—in youth, fresh, ardent, emotional, aspiring, full of adventure; at maturity, brave, perceptive, under control, neither too talkative nor too reticent, neither flippant nor somber; of the bodily figure, the movements easy, the complexion showing the best blood, somewhat flush'd, breast expanded, an erect attitude, a voice whose sound outvies music, eyes of calm and steady gaze, yet capable also of flashing—and a general presence that holds its own in the company of the highest.

As always, his dream of moral and physical perfection was one that even he could not live up to himself. In 1872, he had a falling out with his friend William Douglas O'Connor. The subject was the right of the freed slaves to vote. O'Connor, a staunch abolitionist, insisted that they should be enfranchised immediately, but Whitman felt that they should have some education before they were entrusted with the full responsibility of democracy. Their anger grew so intense that Whitman stormed out of O'Connor's home, and the two men stopped speaking to each other. The poet remained in an agitated state.

While he worked on his writing, he began to experience recurrent dizzy spells and headaches, signs of hypertension. He tried to ignore them, but finally they caught up with him.

Give Me Solitude

Give me the splendid silent sun with all his beams full-
  dazzling ...
Give me solitude, give me Nature, give me again O Nature
  your primal sanities ...
                          * * *
Keep your splendid silent sun,
Keep your woods O Nature, and the quiet places by the
woods ...
Give me faces and streets ... give me comrades and lovers
  by the thousand!

—"Give Me the Splendid Silent Sun"

EARLY IN THE MORNING HOURS of January 23, 1873, Whitman awoke, unable to move his left arm or leg. He had suffered a serious stroke. Eventually friends found him and brought a doctor. A leave of absence from his job was arranged, and months of recuperation followed, during which he was looked after by several close friends, including Peter Doyle and Ellen O'Connor, who did not share her husband's anger with the poet. During this period, Whitman stayed in frequent communication with his mother in Camden, New Jersey, attempting to minimize his problems and write encouragingly of his progress in regaining the use of his limbs. He assured her that his condition was temporary and had not affected his mind at all. But his leg remained burdensome, and he could not talk or listen too long without getting a headache. She also was not feeling very well, and despite Whitman's efforts, their correspondence was tinged with deep melancholy.

A month after Whitman's stroke, while he was attempting his first exhausting efforts to leave his room, both he and his mother were further saddened by the death of his brother Jeff's wife Mattie in St. Louis. They consoled one another long distance, and Whitman kept sending news of his improvement to cheer her up, telling her of his much appreciated carriage rides and a blooming rose bush brought by a friend. He even suggested, as he had when his wounded soldier friends were feeling low, that he might build a little house for the two of them and his brother Eddie. Unhappy in her living situation with her parsimonious son George and his wife Lou, she loved the idea of moving to Washington to be with Whitman and responded in her barely literate English: "i think walt when folks get old like you and me they ought to have a home of their own," and she went on to describe her modest architectural plans.

By April, Whitman had begun to return to his office even

though he wasn't capable of much work. He described his situation to his mother:

> I can write, pretty well, and my mind is clear, but I cannot walk a block, & have no power to do any thing, in lifting or moving any thing in my room, or at my desk—Still I keep good spirits, better far than I would have supposed myself, knowing that I shall get all right in time.

Because of his many bad days, his doctor began to treat his leg with electricity.

Early in May, Whitman's mother's illness grew worse. Her digestion was failing, and she asked that Whitman not send her any more newspapers because reading made her confused. Within a week, she reported that her nervous system was out of order and that she had headaches and trembling spells, and Whitman grew gravely concerned, writing, "Mother, I am afraid you are more unwell than you say—I think about it night & day." Finally on May 20, in spite of his own condition, he made the trip to Camden to visit her. Three days later she died, leaving behind a final note that singled out Whitman:

> farewell my beloved sons farewell I have lived beyond all comfort in this world dont mourn for me my beloved sons and daughters farewell my dear beloved Walter.

Whitman's grief was overwhelming. While the mourners gathered at the funeral, he stayed in a side room, thumping his cane against the floor again and again. A few days later he returned to Washington, where he stayed with friends because he was too depressed to be alone. Finally, it was decided that he would recuperate better in Camden, where his brother George and his sister-in-law Lou could look after him. With Pete's help he packed his belongings, and even though he did not plan to stay in Camden permanently, he decided to burn some of his manuscripts and letters, just in case his condition suddenly worsened. What poems and letters were destroyed this way will never be known; only a few of Doyle's letters to him survive.

George and Lou had never been especially close to Whitman, so he found himself alone much of the time, missing his circle of friends in Washington. To make matters worse, until they moved into a new house they were building, he had to stay in the room where his mother had died, surrounded by her furniture and personal mementos.

He must have felt some comfort when he heard a voice from his past. Fred Vaughan, his young housemate and friend in Brooklyn during the late 1850s, who was now a train engineer, learned of his illness and the death of his mother and wrote to cheer him up:

> I enclose you one of the very many letters I write to you. I think I have written to you at least once a week for the past four years ... I often keep them months before I destroy them. (Shively, *Calamus* 48)

The enclosed letter read, in part:

> Connected with all and yet distinct from all arrises [sic] thee Dear Walt. Walt—my life has turned out a poor miserable failure. I am not a drunkard nor a teetotaler—I am neither honest nor dishonest. I have my family in Brooklyn and I am supporting them.—I never stole, robbed cheate [sic], nor defrauded any person out of anything., and yet I feels [sic] that I have not been honest to myself—my family nor my friends. (Shively, *Calamus* 49)

In another letter, he wistfully described his poverty, living in a rented room with his wife and four sons. He listed the sights of New York that reminded him of his former friend:

> There is never a day passes but what I think of you ... A bale of cotton on the dock ... a ship loading or unloading at the wharf.—a poor man fallen from the roof of a new building ... All—all to me speak of thee Dear Walt.—Seeing them my friend the part thou occupiest in my spiritual nature—I feel assured you will forgive my remissness of me in writing—My love my Walt—is with you always.— (Shively, *Calamus* 50)

Whatever had or had not happened between Whitman and Fred on a physical plane, Whitman had clearly left a permanent impression on Fred, even though it is not likely that Fred knew he had inspired the "Calamus" poems. Perhaps he felt that he would have been truer to his own instincts had he become Whitman's lover, but his family responsibilities made it too late to consider that option, and so, even though he was trapped in a life that didn't feel authentic, he kept a secret place in his heart for the man he had been closest to. He visited Whitman in 1876 and again in 1890. Peter Doyle did the same and stayed in contact with his friend in letters and occasional visits. The old poet was not easily forgotten by the men he loved.

By autumn, Whitman was beginning to feel more like himself, and in the winter he resumed his writing of essays and poems. But he continued to fear that his health might not hold, and early in 1874, for a second time, he burned a large quantity of his manuscripts and letters "to be ready for what might happen." His poetry now became a kind of solace for him. Although it lacked the passion of his earlier verse, it had gained in a somber sort of wisdom. In "Prayer of Columbus," he spoke in the voice of the aged Columbus, ailing, neglected and in want, placating his Creator:

> I will cling fast to Thee, O God, though the waves
>   buffet me;
> Thee, Thee, at least I know.

And then, finding hope in the midst of despair, Columbus sees a shadowy vision of countless ships crossing the ocean and hears himself saluted by "anthems in new tongues."

Although Walt felt like a prophet without honor in his own land, he had begun to receive admiring letters from England. John Addington Symonds, the scholar of classical Greek culture, wrote of his admiration; Bram Stoker wrote a near love letter:

> I write this openly because I feel that with you I must be open.... I only hope we may sometime meet and I shall be able perhaps to say what I cannot write.... You are a true man, and I would like to be one myself, and so I would be towards you as a brother and as a pupil to his master.... I am writing to you because you are different from other men.... I am six feet two inches high and twelve stone weight naked and used to be forty-one or forty-two inches around the chest.... I have a heavy jaw and a big mouth and thick lips—sensitive nostrils—a snubnose and straight hair.... How sweet a thing it is for a strong healthy man with a woman's eyes and a child's wishes to feel that he can speak so to a man who can be if he wishes father and brother and wife to his soul.... But be assured of this, Walt Whitman—that a man of less than half your own age, reared a conservative in a conservative country, and who has always heard your name cried down by the great mass of people who mention it, here felt

his heart leap towards you across the Atlantic and his soul swelling at the words or rather the thoughts.... (Traubel, *IV* 181)

Edward Carpenter, a young English socialist, wrote that *Leaves of Grass* was inspiring many people in England, most of them women, but some of them, like himself, men who loved men:

> Because you have, as it were, given me a ground for the love of men I thank you continually in my heart. (—And others thank you though they do not say so.) For you have made men to be not ashamed of the noblest instinct of their nature. Women are beautiful; but, to some, there is that which passes the love of women. (Traubel, *III* 414)

In America, Whitman did not fare so well. The salary he had been receiving from his job in Washington was finally terminated, and his finances were at a low ebb. An article called "Walt Whitman's Actual American Position," almost certainly by Whitman himself, appeared at this time in Camden's *West Jersey Press*, bemoaning the lack of appreciation of his work and claiming that he had been cheated:

> Whitman's poems in their public reception have fallen still-born in this country. They have been met, and are met today, with the determined denial, disgust and scorn of orthodox American authors, publishers and editors, and in a pecuniary and worldly sense, have certainly wrecked the life of their author ... No established publishing house will yet print his books. Most of the stores will not even sell them ... Worse still ... having left them in charge of book agents in New York City, who, taking advantage of the author's illness and helplessness, have three of them, one

after another, successively thievishly embezzled every dollar of the proceeds!

He sent the clipping to William Rossetti, who had championed his book in London, and Rossetti reprinted it in *The Athenaeum*, which unleashed a controversy. The *London Daily News* attacked the United States for ignoring one of its greatest writers. Some columnists responded that he deserved to be ignored, claiming that the English were more interested in assaulting American culture than they were in supporting Whitman for his own sake. It was even claimed that a man with four children had lost his job in order to give Whitman his former place in the Treasury Department. The only people who rose to his defense were his old friends John Burroughs and William Douglas O'Connor, the latter still not on speaking terms with the poet. The result of the controversy was a good deal of publicity for *Leaves of Grass*, and an increase in the number of orders for the next edition of his book, including one from England's Poet Laureate, Alfred Lord Tennyson.

So Whitman returned to his first love, his book. In 1876, to celebrate America's 100th birthday, he began to prepare the sixth or "Centennial" edition (which is technically the second issue of the second printing of the 1871 fifth edition) to which he decided to add a second volume of mixed poetry and prose, called *Two Rivulets*. The title symbolized the confluence of his thoughts on the subjects of politics and immortality; but as always, the theme of manly love was connected to the other two, this time in the preface:

In my opinion it is by a fervent, accepted development of Comradeship, the beautiful sane affection of man for man, latent in all the young fellows, North and South, East and West ... that the United States of the future ... are to be most effectually welded together, intercalated, anneal'd into a Living Union.

One day while he was working at the print shop, he met a young man named Harry Stafford, who was to become another of the great loves of his life. Stafford was a good-looking man of 18 with dark hair swept across his forehead and fiercely pene-trating eyes. Like Whitman's other loves, he had little education, but he was moodier than the others, and their rela-tionship was a rocky one. Harry's family lived not far from Camden, at White Horse Farm, in Kirkwood, New Jersey, and soon Whitman was a regular visitor there, sleeping with Harry in the attic room. Once again he was drawn from the busy city to the tranquility of the countryside. He would take a chair and walk slowly down the lane in the direction of nearby Timber Creek, stopping to sit down for frequent rests, getting closer to the creek each day. Finally, when he was able to get all the way there, he exulted in the beauty of nature and felt its healing force, strengthening himself by wrestling with young saplings and immersing himself in nature by taking what he called "Adamic" mud baths.

Eventually, his energy was restored, and although he was in his mid-fifties and Harry in his late teens, they cavorted enough to shock Whitman's friends. When John Burroughs invited Whitman to visit his farm in upstate New York, Whitman wrote to him that he would be accompanied by "my (adopted) son" and insisted, "My nephew and I when traveling always share the same room together and the same bed." Burroughs later commented that "they cut up like young boys and annoyed me sometimes."

Whitman continued his pattern of having one close relation-ship while establishing some interest in other men. He developed attachments to two men named Johnston: John, the son of a Philadelphia artist, and Albert, the son of a New York jeweler. He even managed to connect with one of the Staffords' farmhands, Ed Cattell, who wrote to Whitman in his semiliterate style:

> Would Love to see you once moor for it seems an age Since i last met With you down at the pond and a lovely time We had of it to old man
> … i would like to Com up Som Saterday afteroon and Stay all night With you … i love you Walt and Know that my love is returned to.
>   (Katz, *Love* 228-229)

Whitman wrote back, evidently alarmed that Harry might find out:

> Do not come to see me any more at the Stafford family, & do not call there at all any more—Don't ask me why—I will explain to you when we meet…. I want you to keep this to yourself, & not mention it nor this letter to any one … & as to Harry you know how I love him. Ed, you too have my unalterable love, & always shall have. I want you to come up here and see me.

As if his emotional life were not complicated enough, a woman entered the scene. Anne Gilchrist, the widow of an English literary biographer, had found in his verses what she believed to be the man of her dreams, and had begun corresponding with him several years earlier. Her ardor had both mystified and frightened Whitman:

> O, the voice of my Mate: it must be so … I can wait—any time, a lifetime, many lifetimes—I can suffer, I can dare, I

can learn, grow, toil, but nothing in life or death can tear out of my heart the passionate belief that one day I shall hear that voice say to me, "My Mate. The one I so much want. Bride, Wife, indissoluble eternal!" (Allen, 436)

In a later letter, she had added:

I am yet young enough to bear thee children, my darling, if God should so bless me. And would yield my life for this cause with serene joy if it were so appointed, if that were the price for thy having a 'perfect child' ...

He had answered her coolly, saying he had delayed writing because he was too busy:

I am not insensible to your love. I too send you my love. And do you feel no disappointment because I now write so briefly. My book is my best letter, my response, my truest explanation of all. In it I have put my body and spirit. You understand this better and clearer and fuller than anyone else.... Enough that there surely exists so beautiful and a delicate relation, accepted by both of us with joy.

Of course, she had misinterpreted the passion in his verses. She did not realize that when he had written of the urgency of his feelings in such poems as "One Hour to Madness and Joy," he was doubtless speaking of his secret love of men:

O to draw you to me, to plant on you for the first
  time the lips of a determin'd man....
To be absolv'd from previous ties and conventions, I
  from mine and you from yours! ...
To have the gag remov'd from one's mouth

To have the feeling to-day or any day I am sufficient
    as I am....
To escape utterly from others' anchors and holds!
To drive free! to love free! to dash reckless and
    dangerous!
To court destruction with taunts, with invitations!
To ascend, to leap to the heavens of the love
    indicated to me!
To rise thither with my inebriate soul!
To be lost if it must be so!

When he wrote about women, it was with a less passionate, more artificial tone, as if he were adding these passages to counterbalance the poems inspired by men, in order to appear more universal and appeal to a broader audience:

It is I, you women, I make my way,
I am stern, acrid, large, undissuadable, but I love
    you,
I do not hurt you any more than is necessary for you,
I pour the stuff to start sons and daughters for these
    States,
I press with slow rude muscle,
I brace myself effectually, I listen to no entreaties,
I dare not withdraw till I deposit what has so long
    accumulated within me.

He had sent Mrs. Gilchrist a copy of the complete *Leaves of Grass*, which was not available in England, but there was no inscription in it; and at her request, he had occasionally sent her newspapers. Out of remorse for his lack of response to her feelings, when his mother died, he had sent her ring to the English widow, who no doubt considered it an engagement gift, but it had surely not been intended as such. No one in Whitman's circle had ever known him to show an interest in women. Back in 1862, he had met a woman named Ellen Eyre, who had written him a note inviting further contact, but nothing had ever come of it. Another woman had written that she wanted to beget his child on a mountaintop. He had scrawled on the envelope: "? insane asylum." Juliette Beach, whose husband had written a savage review of *Leaves of Grass*, had published a letter praising the book, anonymously signed by "A Woman" and had corresponded with the poet, telling of her love of his spiritual genius. It was probably to keep her at a distance that he had written "Out of the Rolling Ocean the Crowd," comparing the two of them to two droplets of water who were connected because they were part of the same ocean:

> Return in peace to the ocean my love,
> I too am part of that ocean my love, we are not so
>   much separated.

In a letter to Peter Doyle several years earlier, he had joked about his social success with women at a party:

> I also made love to the women, & flatter myself that I cre-
> ated at least one impression—wretch & gay deceiver that I
> am.... You would be astonished, my son, to see the brass &
> coolness, & the capacity of flirtation & carrying on with the
> girls—I would never have believed it of myself.... Of course,
> young man, you understand, it is all on the square. My going
> in amounts to just talking & joking & having a devil of a
> jolly time, carrying on—that's all.

Undaunted by Whitman's coolness toward her, once her ailing mother had died and she was free, Anne Gilchrist wrote that she was planning to resettle with her children in America to be near the man she loved. Sounding unnerved at her aggression, Whitman tried to dissuade her:

> I do not approve your American trans-settlement. I see so many things here you have no idea of—the social, and almost every other kind of crudeness, meagerness here (at least in appearance.)
>
> Don't do anything towards it nor resolve in it nor make any move at all in it without further advice from me. If I should get well enough to voyage, we will talk about it yet in London.

Nonetheless, she arrived with her three grown children in

Anne Gilchrist

Anne Gilchrist, born Anne Borrows in London in 1828, was married to Alexander Gilchrist, a young writer. Anne was well educated and had published several scientific essays as well as a children's book before the death of her husband in 1861. After Alexander's death Anne helped to finish and publish his biography of William Blake. Gilchrist is perhaps even more famous for having fallen in love with poet Walt Whitman, and for having published "A Woman's Estimate of Walt Whitman" (later changed to "An Englishwoman's Estimate of Walt Whitman"), one of the first critical appreciations of *Leaves of Grass*. Prior to moving her family to Philadelphia so as to be nearer to the poet, Gilchrist and Whitman exchanged letters for a number of years, but upon their first meeting, it became obvious to Gilchrist that the relationship would not be a romantic one. Though Whitman was not romantically interested in Gilchrist, as she had hoped he would be, the two formed an intimate and lasting friendship.

September 1876, and moved into a house in Philadelphia, just across the Delaware river from Walt's house in Camden. There, she prepared a guest room especially for Whitman's use, and, dressed in his gray suit with his immaculate white shirt collar, he did occasionally visit her family, sometimes for supper, after which they would take their chairs out to the sidewalk and listen to him converse and recite poetry and sing. Sometimes he would visit for several days, but his relations with her and her family were no more than friendly. His more passionate feelings were still reserved for men, especially for Harry Stafford, and when Mrs. Gilchrist paid a surprise visit to the Staffords' White Horse Farm, he made no effort to hide his angry displeasure.

Whitman's moodiness was familiar to the Staffords. He grew angry when Harry's mother tried to straighten up his papers, but his outbursts of temper lasted only a brief time and were readily forgiven since as an artist, he had a right to be temperamental—and besides he had helped Harry to get a job as a printer. His relationship with young Harry had grown stormy, partly because Harry was uncertain about the nature of their connection, and their emotional turmoil is easily traced in their many letters. Walt gave Harry a ring, this one clearly intended as a symbol of their bond, but Harry returned it when they had a fight, only to ask for it back a month later in the semiliterate prose common to most of Whitman's boyfriends:

> I wish you would put the ring on my finger again, it seems to me there is something that is wanting to complete our friendship when I am with you. I have tride to studdy it out but cannot find out what it is. You know when you put it on there was but one thing to part it from me and that was death. (Shively, *Calamus* 160)

Perhaps it was commitment that was missing in their relationship, or perhaps, despite the fact that they slept together, it was sex that was the missing component. They continued to squabble, and once again Harry wrote for forgiveness:

> I know that it is my falt and not yours. Can you forgive me and take me back and love me the same I will try by the grace of God to do better. I cannot give you up, and it makes me feel so bad to think how we have spent the last day or two, and all for my temper. I will have to control it or it will send me to the States Prison or some other bad place. Cant you take me back and love me the same. Your lovin, but bad-tempered, Harry. (Shively, *Calamus* 151)

His eagerness was clear:

> You may say that I don't care for you, but I do.... I think of you all the time. I want you to come up to-morrow night if you can. I have been to bed to night, but could not sleep fore thinking of you, so I got up and scribbled a few lines to you to go in the morning mail.... You are all the true friend I have and when I cannot have you I will go away some ware, I don't know where. (Shively, *Calamus* 152)

Most likely, it was Harry's fear of being abnormal that created the friction between them. He wrote to Whitman:

> I think of you whenever I have a moment to think ... I am thinking of what I am shielding. I want to try & make a man of myself & do what is right if I can do it.

One of Whitman's loving notes to Harry indicates that their closeness had some physical component:

Dear son, how I wish you could come in now, even if but for an hour & take off your coat, & sit down on my lap—

And Harry wrote of missing Whitman, whose very absence had become a presence in the Stafford home:

I cannot enjoye myself any more at home, if I go up in my room I always come down feeling worse than I do when I go up, for the first thing I see is your picture, and when I come down in the sitting room there hangs the same, and whenever I do anything, or say anything the picture seems to me is always looking at me ... I have [found a girlfriend] and, that is to say, she is a good and true friend to me, we have had many good times together, but none that hangs with me like those you and I have had.(Shively, *Calamus* 162)

In another letter he wrote of wanting to imitate his idol Whitman:

I have been thinking of the suit of cloths which I am to have like yours: I have had myself all pictured out with a suit of gray ..., and a white slouch hat on about fifty times, since you spoke of it; the fellows will call me Walt then. I will have to do something great and good in honor of the name. What will it be? (Shively, *Calamus* 164)

Several years after the period of their greatest stress, when they had begun to drift apart, Whitman gave Harry the highest accolade:

Dear Hank, I realize plainly that *if I had not known you*—if it hadn't been for you & our friendship & my going down there summers to the creek with you—and living there with

your folks ... *I should not be a living man today*—I think &
remember deeply these things & they comfort me—& *you,
my darling boy, are the central figure of them all—*

Stafford wrote a letter two years later, closing "With lots of love
and a good old time kiss I am ever your boy Harry. Write me a
letter soon." (Shively, *Calamus* 171)

For all his passion, Harry finally could not commit himself
to Whitman. Several years later, in 1884, he married Eva
Wescott.

There was no such problem, however, for the young English
socialist, Edward Carpenter, who came to visit Whitman for
the first time in 1877. His life, like that of Anne Gilchrist and
many others, had been changed by reading *Leaves of Grass*. He
stayed for several weeks, during which Whitman brought him
to the Stafford farm and to Mrs. Gilchrist's house. He would
return seven years later.

A second visitor that year was a young Canadian doctor,
Richard Maurice Bucke, who ran a mental hospital in London,
Ontario. Bucke had been greatly inspired by the spirituality of
Whitman's poetry. His first view of the poet, whose work he
had been reading for the past ten years, was overwhelming and
unleashed a powerful mystical experience. The next year, he
invited Whitman to visit him in Ontario. He, too, would write
a book that dealt with his mentor. (Bucke)

Two years later, in 1879, there was a third notable visitor, the
famous poet Henry Wadsworth Longfellow. Whitman was not
at home when Longfellow called, so he had to be looked for at
the docks, where he was riding around on the local boats.
When they finally did meet, the time left was short, and very
little of importance was said. Perhaps Whitman resented
Longfellow as a representative of the New England literary
world that, with the exceptions of Henry David Thoreau,

Bronson Alcott, and Ralph Waldo Emerson, had always turned its back on him, or perhaps Longfellow's sensibility was simply too different from his own, but the two men did not have a pleasurable encounter. Nonetheless, the fact that Longfellow had bothered to make the visit was an indication of Whitman's growing recognition as a major literary figure.

That year, Whitman delivered his first in what would become a sporadic series of lectures on his hero Abraham Lincoln, describing the times he had seen the president and, with the help of Peter Doyle's first-hand account, describing what the scene in Ford's Theater had been like on the night of the assassination. Although he had become a respected figure, reading poetry and speaking at public occasions, Whitman was not a great lecturer. He sat and read his manuscript, and his voice was somewhat constricted. His clear enthusiasm for his subject must have helped, but his powers were beginning to decline.

Also that year, Anne Gilchrist finally gave up her dream of marrying Whitman, left her house in Philadelphia, and, defeated, returned with her children to London.

■ chapter

nine

Good-Bye My Fancy

Good-bye my Fancy!
Farewell dear mate, dear love! ...
The slower fainter ticking of the clock is in me,
Exit, nightfall, and soon the heart thud stopping.
Long have we lived, joy'd, caress'd together;
Delightful!—now separation—
  Good-bye my Fancy.

—"Good-Bye My Fancy!"

IN THE FALL OF 1879, WHITMAN made his longest journey since his 1848 trip to New Orleans. He was asked to speak at the celebration of the 25th anniversary of the state of Kansas, and he traveled by train to Lawrence and Topeka, stopping along the way to visit his brother Jeff and his nieces in St. Louis, Missouri. Then he continued on as far as Denver, Colorado, where he was impressed by the legendary heroic Western character of the men he had long praised in his poetry, although he found the women too imitative of the overly civilized East Coast. At one place he was so busy conversing with the locals that he forgot to give his speech. At other places, he composed fictional interviews for the newspapers. He returned by a more southern route, at last exploring the America whose beauties he had long extolled. But Whitman was growing weaker as he traveled. He stopped to recuperate during a visit with Jeff, a stop that stretched out for three months because he simply did not have the carfare to get home.

Five months after his return, he undertook a second trip, this time to visit Dr. Richard Maurice Bucke at the asylum he ran in London, Ontario. After stopping to admire Niagara Falls, he joined Bucke, observing the asylum inmates with equanimity, and enjoying walks and boat trips. Bucke and he traveled to Montreal and Quebec, and explored the beauties of the Canadian landscape. All the while, Bucke was observing this free-spirited man with silent awe. The following year he would write a biography of the poet, with Whitman, as usual, providing suggestions.

Back in Camden, Whitman discovered that someone had used the printer's plates to publish a pirated edition of *Leaves of Grass*. In a way, considering that the sexuality of his poems was still a controversial topic among literary critics, it was something of a compliment. But Whitman had little money, and the illicit edition denied him revenue that he sorely needed. He was furious, but there was nothing he could do. He must have been relieved, then, when James R. Osgood, a famous publisher, agreed to print a new edition of the *Leaves*, and the poet was able to begin work on the seventh version of his masterpiece. This new version, which appeared in 1881, incorporated all the additions and annexes he had been appending to the original book, so that within a single structure he was finally able to trace his own life's course from youth to adulthood to old age. As he had so confidently exclaimed:

Camerado, this is no book,
Who touches this touches a man,

He still had time to travel, however, and he took pleasure in returning to the scenes of his boyhood in order to help Dr. Bucke with the research for his biography. On a trip to Boston, he was able to visit the ailing Ralph Waldo Emerson, who had once been his supporter, and the grave of Henry David Thoreau, who had visited him in Brooklyn many years earlier and written a glowing description of him.

When the seventh edition of *Leaves of Grass* was officially declared obscene by the Boston District Attorney and banned from the Boston mail unless certain parts were removed, Whitman refused to censor his own work and insisted that it must remain intact. Once again his old friend William Douglas O'Connor forgot their old argument and rose to Whitman's defense in the name of freedom of speech. Finally the ban was lifted, but the publisher, frightened by the episode, decided to sever his connection with the book and sold the printer's plates back to the poet.

Whitman was able to find a new publisher, Rees Welsh & Co., in Philadelphia, and he began to prepare his diaries for publication under the title *Specimen Days*, a volume that contained not only his vivid accounts of his Civil War experiences, but also literary opinions and descriptions of his rural boyhood, his life in the city, his return to the countryside, and the glories of the natural landscape. In *Specimen Days* Whitman shares with his readers his enduring mystical fascination for the seashore. He speaks of his passion for trees, admiring their strength, their beauty, and their imperturbable calm. Nature, one of the main themes throughout his writing, is presented as a healing force:

> I find the woods in mid-May and early June my best places for composition. Seated on logs or stumps there, or resting on rails, nearly all the following memoranda have been jotted down.... After you have exhausted what there is in business, politics, conviviality, love, and so on—have found that none of these finally satisfy, or permanently wear—what remains? Nature remains; to bring out from their torpid recesses, the affinities of a man or woman with the open air, the trees, fields, the changes of seasons—the sun by day and the stars of heaven by night.

In a footnote, he describes his hope that his work will reach those who may be helped by it:

> Who knows, (I have it in my fancy, my ambition,) but the pages now ensuing may carry ray of sun, or smell of grass or corn, or call of bird, or gleam of stars by night, or snow-flakes falling fresh and mystic, to denizen of heated city house, or tired workman, or workwoman?—or may-be in sick-room or prison—to serve as cooling breeze, or Nature's aroma, to some fever'd mouth or latent pulse.

Whitman's work was still inspiring others. Early in 1882, he was visited by the young Irish playwright Oscar Wilde, whose brilliant wit had already brought him international acclaim. Wilde was an urbane sophisticate living in London, who arrived in Camden dressed in a brown velvet suit to pay his respects to the simply dressed "Good Gray Poet." Like other homosexuals in England, he had been inspired by the open proclamations of sexuality in Whitman's verse, and he saw Whitman as the herald of a new era. He sat on a low stool with

The Sentencing Statement Against Oscar Wilde

Justice Wills: Oscar Wilde and Alfred Taylor, the crime of which you have been convicted is so bad that one has to put stern restraint upon one's self to prevent one's self from describing, in language which I would rather not use, the sentiments which must rise in the breast of every man of honor who has heard the details of these two horrible trials. That the jury has arrived at a correct verdict in this case I cannot persuade myself to entertain a shadow of a doubt; and I hope, at all events, that those who sometimes imagine that a judge is half-hearted in the cause of decency and morality because he takes care no prejudice shall enter into the case, may see that it is consistent at least with the utmost sense of indignation at the horrible charges brought home to both of you.

It is no use for me to address you. People who can do these things must be dead to all sense of shame, and one cannot hope to produce any effect upon them. It is the worst case I have ever tried. That you, Taylor, kept a kind of male brothel it is impossible to doubt. And that you, Wilde, have been the center of a circle of extensive corruption of the most hideous kind among young men, it is equally impossible to doubt.

I shall, under the circumstances, be expected to pass the severest sentence that the law allows. In my judgment it is totally inadequate for a case such as this. The sentence of the Court is that each of you be imprisoned and kept to hard labor for two years.

his hand on Whitman's knee, and in spite of the vast social differences between them, the two men got along famously. Wilde, who was used to the finest wines, gladly drank the homemade elderberry wine that he was offered, and when his traveling companion later commented that drinking it must have been difficult for him, he replied, "If it had been vinegar, I would have drunk it all the same, for I have an admiration for that man which I can hardly express." Wilde added, "He is the grandest man I have ever seen, the simplest, most natural and strongest character I have ever met in my life.... The kiss of Walt Whitman is still on my lips." (Allen, 502)

Fifteen years later (after Whitman had denied his homosexuality in response to John Addington Symonds' letter), Wilde rashly sued his lover Bosie Douglas's father, the Marquis of Queensberry, for calling him a sodomite, and when the court found that the accusation was true, Wilde landed in jail, a broken man. Almost as soon as the subculture of gay men began to become visible, there were some members of traditional society who were ready to persecute its practitioners.

But the gate had nonetheless been opened. Two years after Wilde's visit, young Bram Stoker, who had written a passionate letter to Whitman a decade earlier, also visited along with Henry Irving, the actor he managed, and both men established an enduring friendship with Whitman. Whitman also had a circle of friends, acquaintances and supporters among the professional people of Philadelphia, but polite society never became as fully satisfying to him as the companionship of simple, virile young men.

In 1884, when his brother George moved to a new home out in the country, Whitman decided he wanted to stay in town. He was able to purchase with his meager savings a small house at 328 Mickle Street (now 330 Mickle Boulevard) in Camden, and at last he could entertain his visitors without imposing on his sister-in-law Lou, but George was insulted and stopped talking to Whitman for several years. The house had two stories, with a kitchen, dining room, small bedroom, and sitting room on the first floor, and three bedrooms on the second. From his room, surrounded by unruly piles of papers and manuscripts and books, Whitman could hear the nearby trains, which doubtless reminded him of the young railroad men he had always admired. When the wind blew the wrong way, he had to put up with the smell of guano from a nearby fertilizer factory, and on Sundays he had to endure the loud bells and overenthusiastic choir from a neighborhood church. But for the first time in his life he was no longer a boarder or a tenant or a guest. He had a home of his own.

One of the earliest visitors to Mickle Street was Edward Carpenter, the Englishman who had visited him seven years earlier. Carpenter stayed with Whitman, and, like Dr. Bucke before him, he idolized the poet enough to spend much of his time observing Whitman's activities and manners, turning his notes into a book called *Days With Walt Whitman*, which he published several years after the poet's death. (Carpenter) It wasn't until he was an old man himself and went to bed with a young man named Gavin Arthur, the grandson of President Chester Alan Arthur, that Carpenter revealed that he had been to bed with Whitman, who had spent the night worshipfully caressing the young Englishman's entire body. (Arthur, 132–33) At first Carpenter said in a conversation with Arthur that he believed that Whitman was bisexual. Arthur reports that he asked in a conversation with Carpenter:

"Do you think he liked women too—I mean in bed?"

"Yes, especially when he was young and bursting with potency ....

But after he got that infection during his hospital work in

your Civil War, and he knew he might not be potent enough to satisfy women, I think he was more at ease, in bed at least, with his men friends....Essentially he was bisexual ...”

(Arthur, 136–37)

Arthur originally omitted the fact that Carpenter's own love-making—an imitation of Whitman's—had brought him to the point of physical orgasm, but after Arthur's death, the information was released. (Katz, *Love* 324-327) Carpenter himself altered his original assessment of Whitman as bisexual and in 1922 stated, "There is no doubt in my mind that before all, Whitman was a lover of the Male." (Katz, *History* 365)

When his stroke-induced lameness made it too difficult for Whitman to manage the house on his own, he invited a series of people in to help. The first, a married couple named Lay, didn't last very long. He then asked a widow named Mary Oakes Davis to be his housekeeper. She was a neighbor with a history of looking after people who were old, ill, or blind, and even of taking in their orphaned children. She had already been helping Whitman with cooking and mending and tending his house, so at his request she moved in her furniture and pets and devoted herself to looking after him, even paying for some expenses and repairs out of her own pocket.

Whitman's health began to decline, and after suffering sun-stroke in 1885, he found it almost impossible to get around. The friends who had been enlisted to look after him collected money from 32 people—including such notable figures as the writers Mark Twain, John Greenleaf Whittier, and Oliver Wendell Holmes, and the actor Edwin Booth—to buy him a horse and carriage. When it was presented to him, he was so moved that he wept, and he was able to get considerable use out of it for the next several years.

Bill Duckett, who was boarding with Mrs. Davis, often

accompanied him on his rides and became the first of a series of young male companions who tended to the poet's needs in his final years, sawing wood for the fireplace and carrying it upstairs, doing carpentry repairs on the house, shoveling snow, running errands, and wheeling Whitman through the streets in a chair when he could no longer walk. (He tried one female nurse, Elizabeth Leavitt Keller, but was unable to get along with her. Nonetheless, she managed to produce a book about what a burden he was for his caretakers.) His last attendant was a handsome, mustachioed young seaman named Warren Fritzinger, an adopted ward of Mrs. Davis.

At the end of 1885, Whitman received news that his longtime admirer, Anne Gilchrist, had died in England, and although he had rejected her, her loss was painful to him. Believing that he didn't have long to live, in 1886 he had paintings of himself done by Herbert Gilchrist (Anne's son), Thomas Eakins, and J.W. Alexander, as well as a bust by Sidney Morse.

At the end of March 1888, Whitman suffered another stroke, which nearly killed him, but he began to recuperate several months later. It was at this time that an admirer named Horace Traubel, a married man in his thirties, began to visit Whitman daily. Despite his marriage, Traubel formed deep emotional—and possibly physical—attachments to other men, as witnessed by his friendship with the artist Marsden Hartley, known to be homosexual, documented in their letters during the early years of the 20th century:

> I count myself heaven blessed with your precious love and ask no more than to walk on throughout the exquisite days with you.... It is enough that you call me brother, friend, lover.

It is doubtful that there was anything physical in Traubel's relationship with Whitman, especially considering the poet's poor health, but Traubel did become the last great comrade of Whitman's life. In his daily visits, he took notes on all the conversations that his friend had with himself and others, creating a scrupulously detailed record of Whitman's final four years, including everything from his opinions on the great poets to his complaints about his digestion. Almost all of it has been printed under the title "*With Walt Whitman in Camden,*" a total of nine hefty volumes.

Whitman had been working on a new volume of poems to be called *November Boughs*, and Traubel helped him to ready the manuscript for the printer. The slim volume began with a preface called "A Backward Glance O'er Traveled Roads," in which Whitman assessed his literary career:

> I look upon *Leaves of Grass*, now finished to the end of its opportunities and powers, as my definitive *carte visite* to the coming generations of the New World ... from a worldly and business point of view *Leaves of Grass* has been worse than a failure ... I had my choice when I commenced. I bid neither for soft eulogies, big money returns, nor the approbation of existing schools and conventions.... I consider the point that I have positively gain'd a hearing, to far more than make up for any and all other lacks and withholdings. Essentially, that was from the first, and has remain'd throughout, the main object.

Calling his book an experiment, he seemed to want to take back some of his brave words:

> I have unwittingly ... made an attempt at such statements— which I certainly would not assume to do now, knowing more clearly what it means.

November Boughs was added to the limited edition of Whitman's *Complete Poems & Prose*, which became the eighth edition of *Leaves of Grass*. His poetic powers had for the most part waned by this time:

> Thanks in old age—thanks ere I go ...
> For precious ever-lingering memories, (of you my
> mother dear—you, father—you, brothers,
> sisters, friends,) ...
> For all the brave strong men—devoted, hardy men—
> who've forward sprung in freedom's help ...

In his final few years, life was not as splendid as he had once announced: "Old age superbly rising! O welcome, ineffable grace of dying days!" He was mostly confined to his home, visited by loyal friends, and very rarely able to go to a dinner to honor him or to deliver a final Lincoln lecture. He stayed mostly in his upstairs bedroom in the oak bedstead made by his father, underneath which a large round metal tub was kept for bathing him. He was in this condition when he received the letter from his English admirer, John Addington Symonds, asking whether he might "contemplate the intrusion of those semi-sexual emotions and actions which no doubt do occur between men," inspired by the reading of his poems.

Surely he thought about the men in his life as he made his decision: not only Peter Doyle, but Fred Vaughan, the soldiers Lewy Brown and Tom Sawyer, Harry Stafford, Horace Traubel and the many briefer contacts with men like Ed Cattell and Jack Flood and all those in the lengthy lists in his daybooks. And perhaps he thought of those he had inspired from afar: Oscar Wilde, Edward Carpenter, Bram Stoker, and of the generations of men yet to read his words and be encouraged by them.

His beloved Peter Doyle may not have understood Whitman's poetry, but in an interview he revealed that he did understand Whitman's ambition:

> Walt often spoke to me of his book. I would tell him, "I don't know what you are trying to get at." And this is the idea I would always arrive at from his reply. All other peoples in the world have had their representatives in literature: here is a great big race with no representative. He would undertake to furnish that representative. It was also his object to get a real human being into a book. This had never been done before. These were the two things he tried to impress upon me every time we talked of books—especially of his book. (Shively, *Calamus* 118)

There was a human being in *Leaves of Grass*, perhaps not a totally honest man, but certainly one who deserved to be heard. If that man were to have any future—especially since the poet believed that the book had failed in its own time—he could not afford to be burdened with an anomalous sexuality. First he must survive, in order to be heard at all. Then, when his voice had been heard, those who felt as he had would understand its message in their special way, and perhaps in the society of their time they would be able to freely express their feelings. And so perhaps he invented six fictional children and denied some of his deepest feelings, in order that his one true child, his book, might live.

During his last year, Whitman designed the tomb that would hold his own remains and those of his closest family members. Despite his pain, he still managed to publish a second annex to *Leaves of Grass* entitled after its lovely final poem, "Good-bye My Fancy!" At the end, he authorized the completed form of his life-long work, folding the last annex into the seventh and final version, known as the "deathbed edition" of 1892. On March 26, 1892, he uttered his final words, asking his attendant Warren Fritzinger to shift him in his bed: "Warry, turn."

A death notice was posted on the door to inform the many friends and admirers that the Good Gray Poet had died. The official causes were pleurisy, tuberculosis, and nephritis, and the doctors expressed amazement that his constitution had been strong enough to allow him to survive so long with so many tubercular lesions throughout his internal organs.

Whitman left most of his modest estate to his handicapped brother Eddie, who survived him by only eight months. He left small amounts to his sisters and to his housekeeper Mrs. Davis (who later sued the estate for more). In an earlier will, he had left his gold watch to Harry Stafford and a silver one to Peter Doyle, but in his final will, the gold watch went to Horace Traubel and the silver one to Stafford.

The house was open for three hours so that the public could view the coffin, and several thousand viewers streamed through before it was taken in a procession to Harleigh Cemetery. Peter Doyle arrived late and was almost turned away, but someone recognized him in time to let him say farewell to his dearest old comrade. Several years later in an interview, Pete said that he had kept Whitman's old overcoat:

> I have Walt's raglan here. I now and then put it on, lay down, think I am in the old times. Then he is with me again. It's the only thing I kept among many old things. When I get it on and stretch out on the old sofa I am very well contented. It is like Aladdin's lamp. I do not ever for a minute lose the old man. He is always nearby. When I am in trouble—in a crisis—I ask myself, "What would Walt have done under these circumstances?" and whatever I decide Walt would have done, that I do." (Shively, *Calamus* 119)

The Real Me

Oppress'd with myself that I have dared to open my
* mouth,*
Aware now that amid all that blab whose echoes recoil
* upon me I have not once had the least idea who or*
* what I am,*
But that before all my arrogant poems the real Me
* stands yet untouch'd, untold, altogether unreach'd ...*
                     —"As I Ebb'd with the Ocean of Life"

OVER THE DECADES SINCE HIS death the understanding of Whitman's sexual nature has been continually revised. Right after the first publication of *Leaves of Grass*, Rufus Griswold attacked the poet, accusing him of "the horrible sin not to be named among Christians" (homosexuality). (Warner xxvi) Protective friends depicted him instead as an asexual, saintly figure: Dr. Bucke, in his *Cosmic Consciousness* went as far as to rank him with Jesus, Buddha, and Mohammed as forerunners of a new stage in the evolution of the human mind. (Bucke, 311, 318) In 1905, a German critic, Eduard Bertz, again raised the issue of Whitman's unorthodox sexuality (Duberman, 95, n7), but the biographers of that time, such as Bliss Perry resisted the idea:

> There is also abundant evidence that from 1862 onward his life was stainless so far as sexual relations were concerned ... to conceive of Walt Whitman as an habitual libertine, even in his youth, is to misunderstand his nature. (Perry 46, 47)

Again in 1913, Dr. W.C. Rivers, in his *Walt Whitman's Anomaly*, openly accused the poet of homosexuality.

> Walt Whitman's personal character is ... typical of the male invert. If ever one had the woman's soul in the man's body, it was he. In almost everything except outward form he was a woman. (Duberman, 85)

Although this occasioned some discussion at the time, the subject was dropped, and scholars continued to sweep it under the rug, even if that meant ignoring their own findings. In 1920, Emory Holloway discovered that the original draft of Whitman's New Orleans poem, "Once I Pass'd Through a Populous City," was actually about an affair with a man rather than a woman (Holloway, "WW's Love Affairs" 477), and had once read:

> I remember I say only that man who passionately clung
>   to me ...
> Again he holds me by the hand, I must not go,

But Holloway elected to ignore his own findings in a biography he published in 1926, surmising that Whitman lost his editorship because of a heterosexual affair:

> Or perhaps the owners of the *Crescent* had heard the gossip going around among the newspaper men that Whitman had taken up with a woman, one of the class at once most fascinating and most accessible, an octoroon.... That Whitman was no stranger to woman is evident to any reader of his verse. (Holloway, *Whitman* 65)

There is a particular wistfulness in the knowledge that this love had to be kept secret. If it had been an affair with an "octoroon" woman, fear of racial prejudice would have made it necessary to hide from the prejudices of antebellum America. But if it was an affair with a man of any color, it would not only have had to be hidden, it would have affected the poet's sense of masculinity and normality. His departure from New Orleans could not simply leave behind a societal problem, for he had to take with him forever the awareness of his own participation in this forbidden love affair and its significance: his very self-definition.

Much of our understanding of the process by which Whitman hid his sexual nature stems from our awareness of his changes in pronouns. In an effort to avoid censure and relegation to the margins of American literature, he did his best to cover his tracks by encoding his love of men as a desire for women or for wholesome "comradeship." But the controversy grew nonetheless, and for nearly a century, critics argued back and forth about what his real sexuality was and how it affected our understanding of his work.

The theme of "Once I Pass'd Through a Populous City" is a love affair and a separation, no matter what the gender of the lover. As Robert K. Martin points out in *The Homosexual Tradition in American Poetry*:

> What matters for a literary critic is the text, not the life. But when two texts exist ... it is certainly valid to ask why the change was made and if the change can be traced to aesthetic considerations.... Whitman's own life was marked by the same pressures toward social conformity that now lead to critical distortions.... The changing of texts, the excision of passages, are but the most obvious of what must have been an enormously painful series of acts performed almost daily to conform to someone else's version of normality. (Martin, 4, 7)

Critics, in order to complete their understanding, would do well to analyze the work within the context of the artist's life, but for the "New Criticism" of the 1940s and 50s, and for the Postmodernists of the 1980s and 90s, the author's life is irrelevant. Only what is on the page is important. The biographer, unlike the critic, however, has a legitimate interest in the life itself and how it illuminates the work. And in Whitman's case, since the poetry purports to be the life of the poet ("Who holds this book holds a man"), it is all the more important to study the source material that is the basis of the poems.

The fascination with Whitman's sexual life continued to grow in spite of Holloway's omission. D.H. Lawrence included an essay on Whitman in his *Studies in Classic American Literature* of 1923. Himself a writer censored for his depictions of (hetero)sexual love, he saw that Whitman's lines about sex with women did not ring true because they lacked passion:

> "A woman waits for me—" He might as well have said: "The femaleness waits for my maleness." Oh, beautiful generalization and abstraction! Oh biological function.... "Athletic mothers of these States—" Muscles and wombs. They needn't have had faces at all. (Lawrence, 176)

He admired the poet's visionary theme of setting the free soul out on the "Open Road" of life, and he called it "the bravest doctrine man has ever proposed to himself" (Lawrence, 183), but he felt that Whitman didn't quite succeed in his noble dream because his desire to "merge" or empathize with others, especially with his comrades, would lead to homosexuality, a love which he apparently considered barren and ultimately morbid:

Whitman's Notebooks

Often using typical writer's notebooks, Walt Whitman jotted down thoughts, lists, lines of poetry, and notes for lectures. During the civil war years, he often kept notes on the wounded soldiers he visited and the requests they made. Thomas Harned, one of Whitman's close friends and literary executors, donated some 40 such notebooks to the Library of Congress. It is estimated that Whitman created over 100 of these notebooks, many of which are collected in libraries at numerous universities. Images from Whitman's notebooks can be viewed at the library of congress website (*http://memory.loc.gov/ammem/wwhtml/wwcoll.html*), while images of his poetry can be seen at the Walt Whitman archive (*www.whit-manarchive.org/*).

> For the great mergers, woman at last becomes inadequate....
> So the next step is the merging of man-for-man love. And
> this is on the brink of death. It slides over into death....
> Death is not the *goal.* And Love, and merging, are now only
> part of the death process. Comradeship—part of the death
> process. Democracy—part of the death process. (Lawrence,
> 178, 179)

For Lawrence, the ideal of democracy is fulfilled only when all
souls (citizens) are independent, but for Whitman it is spiritual
*inter*dependence that makes a democratic community, and that
interdependence is based on the love of comrades. Male–male
love is not responsible for the existence of death. Death is part
of the life process, and as such is something to be accepted and
even celebrated, not feared and detested.

Critics who exhibited what we now call "homophobia"
believed that writers from a sexual minority had nothing of
value to say to the rest of humanity. Mark Van Doren again
raised the issue of Whitman's homosexuality in a negative way
in 1935, in a piece called "Walt Whitman, Stranger," and three
years later, Newton Arvin, in his biography called *Whitman,*
courageously took him on, asserting the Good Gray Poet's sexuality without apology and defending the value of his poems:

> ... Mr. Mark Van Doren has pointed out that what Whitman
> half-consciously meant by "manly attachment" was not
> simply a normal brotherly feeling among men but homo-
> sexual love ... and as such has no serious meaning ... for
> healthy men and women.... For one thing the fact of
> Whitman's homosexuality is one that cannot be denied by
> any informed and candid reader of the "Calamus" poems, of
> his published letters, and of accounts by unbiased acquain-
> tances: after a certain point the fact stares one unanswerably

in the face.... Does all this mean, however, that Whitman's whole prophecy as a democratic poet ... is invalidated by having its psychological basis in a sexual aberration? ... He chose to translate and sublimate his strange, anomalous emotional experience into a political, a constructive, a democratic program. In doing so, he made himself the voice of something far larger and more comprehensive than his own private sensibility. (Lawrence, 273–275)

The atmosphere of homophobia grew so powerful, however, that two decades later, Newton Arvin was arrested for possession of male pornography, removed from his teaching duties, and sent to a mental hospital.

A sad note is that some critics who themselves were later revealed to be gay, perhaps in order to deflect accusations against themselves, also joined in the denunciation and trivialization of Whitman's work. According to Whitman scholar Betsy Erkkila, the noted Americanist F.O. Matthiessen, himself homosexual, wrote to his lover Russell Chaney sympathetically about Whitman's attachments to men (Erkkila, 168, n3), yet in 1941, in his famous study *American Renaissance,* he called Whitman's work, "vaguely pathological and homosexual" and claimed that his primary value was in his "language experiment." (Matthiessen, 517–605) Matthiessen committed suicide in 1950. (Bergman, 85) Similar to Matthieson, Malcolm Cowley wrote in private to his male lover about Whitman's themes of homosexuality and democracy, but when he published a 1959 introduction to a reprint of the 1855 edition, he focused almost exclusively on the poet's spirituality, noting only in passing Whitman's "ambiguous doctrine of male comradeship." (Cowley, xxxi)

In 1943 the subject appeared again when Henry Seidel Canby acknowledged the significance of Whitman's sexuality, but concluded that it could not be evaluated because we could never know about it with certainty:

> ... Walt ... records in his private notebooks perturbations of unsatisfied passion, and writes in his letters to young soldiers of a love which is more than friendship. That this ... living personality is unimportant, critically and biographically, is, of course, nonsense.... No biographer can follow Whitman's lead and omit from his life whatever does not seem appropriate in the background of a prophet and bard of democracy. Unfortunately, much has to be omitted because we simply have no facts, and in all probability never will have. (Canby, 187)

Yet without facts, Canby went on to "diagnose" Whitman on the basis of his poetry. Since he decided, despite all the love letters and all the lists of men, that "there has been, so far, been educed not one scrap of evidence of actual homosexuality in Whitman's life," Canby concluded that the poet was "a narcissist," "in love with himself," a creature of "auto-eroticism" (not to be confused with masturbation) "in love with his own body." (Canby, 199–203)

Most writers continued to disparage this central area of Whitman's sensibility. The primary biography of the 1950s was Gay Wilson Allen's meticulously researched compendium of factual information on Whitman's life, *The Solitary Singer*, which remains the most useful source of hard data on the poet. On the subject of Whitman's sexuality, Allen concluded— largely on the basis of the poet's tortured diary entry about Peter Doyle in 1870—that although Whitman's desires were probably homosexual, "The important fact is not his affection for men like Lewis Brown, Thomas Sawyer, and Peter Doyle, but his struggle for self-control and self understanding." (Allen,

424) When Martin Duberman, in a review of a television program on Whitman, singled out Allen's *Solitary Singer* as an example of gay experience being written out of history, Allen replied in a letter to *The New York Times* of January 11, 1976:

> ... In numerous places I discuss Whitman's deep homoerotic emotions. But I did not detail all the men the poet "slept" with, or state that he slept with them to engage in sodomy. That he may have I nowhere denied, but no detective broke into the room to record the act, ... I think a biographer should go as far as his facts permit, but not to state as positive truth what took place in the dark of night without more evidence than Whitman's ambiguous words "slept with" ... Whitman was not consistently a textbook example of a homosexual—perhaps no one is. (Duberman, 94)

As a forerunner of the liberation of American culture from the vestiges of Victorian prudery, Leslie Fiedler, at the 100th anniversary of the 1855 publication of *Leaves of Grass*, explored with great insight the layers of masks worn by the poet, including an honest examination of the role of his homosexuality:

> As a deliverer of verse from sexual taboos ... willing to be abused and abandoned to redeem the phallus and the orgasm to the imagination, Whitman deserves the credit he has been given.... Those who would preserve this legend of Whitman as the spokesman for total physical love find themselves in the uncomfortable position of having to underestimate the role of homosexuality in his verse.... even his homosexuality is necessary, not publicly proclaimed, but unconsciously *there* for his disciples as well as for himself. (Fiedler, 61, 62)

The tide had begun to turn. Even before the creation of the modern Gay Liberation movement, more writers were taking the risk of speaking openly—and approvingly—of Whitman's homosexuality. In *The Evolution of Walt Whitman*, first published in 1960, French critic Roger Asselineau devoted one volume to the poet's life and a second volume to his work. He dealt with Whitman's homosexuality and its impact on the "Calamus" poems of the third (1860) edition of *Leaves of Grass* in a wholesome, nonjudgmental way:

> It seems probable that a brief homosexual affair had given him a revelation of love and also of the abnormal character of his desires.... Although these admissions were veiled, they touched nonetheless on a subject that had never before been treated with so much frankness, and it required great courage—or an extremely pressing need for confession—for Whitman to dare to celebrate these forbidden desires and joys. In spite of the fact that he had already been criticized for obscenity in his two previous editions, he still persisted in the course he had chosen. This stubbornness clearly shows the importance which he attached to the sexual theme. (Asselineau, 122)

It wasn't until 1969 that the riots at the Stonewall Inn in Greenwich Village sparked a new attitude among gay men and lesbians. Where once their organizations had been content to seek freedom from censure and violence, now there was a political demand for freedom from exploitation and discrimination, an insistence on equality. The street demonstrations of gay activists emboldened homosexuals of every stripe, including scholars. Before long there was a movement toward Gay and Lesbian Studies (later called Queer Studies), and for the first time, gay people began to claim their own history. No longer were literature scholars and historians content to let the accomplishments of their heroes be defined by others. American authors such as Henry James, Emily Dickinson, Willa Cather, Herman Melville—and especially Walt Whitman—were now openly and proudly declared to be the forebears of the new gay culture.

In the 1970s gay historians and critics began to make their case that not only was Whitman homosexual, but that his homosexuality was a positive influence on his work. Bit by bit they reinterpreted the evidence. Jonathan Ned Katz's *Gay American History* examined Whitman's diary entries about going home with men in the 1860s. (Katz, *Gay* 499) His later book, *Love Stories*, gives an expanded account of Whitman's sexual life in a carefully constructed context of the nature of male sexuality and homosexual identity in the 19th century:

> Looking back, it is possible for us to see sexuality in relationships that may not have been perceived then as erotic. Some 19th century authors were aware of the lust inhabiting their love, but they wrote with confidence that their readers would not understand that lust as lust. Some men of the 19th century were perfectly conscious of and even at ease with the lust inhabiting their love. (Katz, *Love* 334)

Charley Shively, in his *Calamus Lovers*, published valuable source material related to Whitman. He was the first to name Fred Vaughan as the object of Whitman's infatuation of the late 1850s (Shively, *Calamus* 36–50), but he impishly portrayed the poet almost as if he were a liberated gay male of the 1970s, leading a wildly promiscuous life, and he even playfully gave male lovers credit for the invention of bathing! (Shively, *Calamus* 37) This was a risky form of humor in the time when gay scholars were seeking to be taken seriously so that their ideas would be accepted after nearly a century of obfuscation, but it seems to have done no harm, and indeed added a refreshing note of self-confidence to the discussion.

Gary Schmidgall, in *Walt Whitman: A Gay Life*, compared his own 20th century gay man's life to Whitman's 19th century life, searching for similarities in their different experiences of themselves, for example comparing Whitman's admiration of the soprano Maria Alboni with modern gay male diva-worship. (Schmidgall, 16)

Eve Kosofsky Sedgwick, celebrated as a groundbreaking figure by postmodernist Queer Studies scholars, delineated Whitman's effect on the English, specifically on Edward Carpenter, Oscar Wilde, John Addington Symonds, and D.H. Lawrence. (Sedgwick, 201–217)

Although it became difficult to deny Whitman's homosexuality after the advent of Queer Studies, some critics remained less friendly to the gay perspective and applied Freudian theory to find the source of Whitman's work in unresolved family conflicts and immature masturbatory practices. (Cavitch, xiii) Some adjusted their emphases to suit their purposes. Justin Kaplan, for example, gave three pages to Whitman's seven-year relationship with Peter Doyle and twenty-seven pages to his two-year relationship with Anne Gilchrist. Later, in his detailed study of the sexual nature of Whitman's work, *Masculine Landscapes*, Byrne Fone took Kaplan to task:

> Kaplan goes on to suggest that "maybe it doesn't matter" what "Whitman actually 'did' with Peter Doyle and the others." Of course it does matter, and saying that it doesn't is another example of the critical trivialization of homosexual sex and desire. (Fone, 16)

Kaplan later admitted in an essay called "The Biographer's Problem" that:

> The history of over a century of Whitman biography is to a large extent the history of a pussyfooting accommodation to the issue of sexuality and, more specifically, homosexuality. One sees biography being skewed in the interest of literary public relations. (Kaplan, *Biographer's* 22)

Paul Zweig, in his biography subtitled *The Making of the Poet*, dealt primarily with Whitman's early years and attempted to explain the poet's references to sexual experiences as the product of unfulfilled fantasies, or even of hallucinogenic drugs! (Zweig 298, 304)

As late as 1995, David S. Reynolds attempted to bring the discussion back to its earlier footing by making the issue once again general and vague in his detailed *Walt Whitman's America: A Cultural Biography*:

> As for his relations with men, they can be best understood as especially intense manifestations of the kind of same-sex passion that was seen everywhere in antebellum America.... Overt displays of affection between people of the same sex were common.... Gender roles, in other words, were fluid, elastic, shifting in a time when sexual types had not yet solidified. No one embodied this fluidity in sexual outlook more than Whitman. (Reynolds, 198–99)

In 1999, Jerome Loving continued in this strain in *Walt Whitman: The Song of Himself*:

> One of the problems with thinking Whitman a homosexual, however, is that we are more than a century removed from a

period in which close male friendship was taken at face value. (Loving, 48)

He brings the subject up in 26 other locations in his book, each time explaining it away.

One is tempted to ask why so much effort has been expended by so many critics in denying and defending the simple truth. If gay scholars are accused of declaring Whitman homosexual for political purposes, can those antipathetic to the gay reading be so resistant for any less political a motive? The more complicated the scholarly discussion gets, the more likely it is that the real Walt Whitman will be lost in the shuffle, which is probably exactly what the poet intended when he set out to craft a fictional image of himself. For if the author remains elusive in some ways, we are forced to pay more attention to his work.

afterword

I believe a leaf of grass is no less than the journey-work of the stars.

—"Song of Myself"

IT HAS BEEN A LITTLE MORE than a century since Walt Whitman's death, and in that time his image has continually grown and changed in the mind of America and the world. He has become many different men to many different readers, and even those who love him most love him for different reasons and do not agree on who he really was. Because his vision was mystical, the Hindus of India see him as a proponent of their religion; and because he was such an ardent admirer of laborers, the communists of the Soviet Union saw him as a champion of the working class. Because he believed in democracy and the preservation of the Union, generations of schoolteachers have focused on his patriotism and his passion for Abraham Lincoln; and because he tended to the wounded of the Civil War, many see him as a saintly nurturer. Because he wrote openly of love between men, some critics have denounced him as a pervert. Some have tried to obscure and minimize the eroticism in his work in order to protect him from charges of immorality and degeneracy, while still others have declared him to be an icon of homosexual liberation.

Of course, he was all these things and more. The one thing there is little argument about is his stature as America's most influential poet. A statue of him stands on Bear Mountain in New York State. Such major figures as Hart Crane, Carl Sandburg, and Allen Ginsberg are clearly inheritors of his poetic style and sensibility. *Visiting Walt* (2003), edited by Sheila Coghill and Thom Tammaro, and *Walt Whitman: The Measure of His Song* (1981, 1998), edited by Jim Perlman, Ed Folsom, and Dan Campion, are anthologies of many of the poems and essays by poets who have been influenced by Whitman. Often they speak in direct address to his departed spirit.

Federico Garcia Lorca confided in "Ode to Walt Whitman":

Not a single moment, old beautiful Walt Whitman,

Have I stopped seeing your beard full of butterflies.
   (Perlman, et al. 159)

In a pessimistic mood, Louis Simpson said in "Walt Whitman at Bear Montain":

Where are you, Walt?
The Open Road leads to the used-car lot. (Perlman, et al. 272)

Allen Ginsberg playfully, yet wistfully, wrote in "A Supermarket in California":

I saw you, Walt Whitman, childless, lonely old grubber, poking among the meats in the refrigerator and eyeing the grocery boys. (Perlman, et al. 213).

And Mark Doty empathizes in "Letter to Walt Whitman":

I hope this finds you. I know you've been bothered
all century, poets lining up
to claim lineage.   (Coghill and Tammaro, 39)

Dozens of biographies and scores of books analyzing Whitman's work have been published, and the *Walt Whitman Quarterly Review* regularly publishes scholarly articles dealing with his life and writing. His life has also been turned into fiction four times: William Douglas O'Connor's *The Carpenter* (1868), which portrays him as a Christ figure, was the first. The others are: Grant Overton's *The Answerer* (1921), John Erskine's *The Start of the Road* (1938), and Ben Aronin's *Walt Whitman's Secret* (1955)—*not* his homosexuality. Two films, both starring Rip Torn as Whitman, have been made: one for television, *Song of Myself* (1976), a retrospective dramatization of some key moments in his life, focusing on his relationship with Peter Doyle, and one for theaters, *Beautiful Dreamers* (1992), the story of his visit with Dr. Bucke in Ontario. A documentary on the poet is part of the video series *Voices and Visions*. Several documentary plays by writers such as Jonathan Ned Katz and actors such as Dan Barshay have been composed from his letters, diaries, and poems.

Whoever Whitman actually was, he has become an American icon, albeit a controversial one. A bridge, a shopping mall, a school, and a poetry center are named for him, despite the opposition of church leaders who perceived him as an immoral libertine. In the early 1990s, a public service announcement aimed at giving gay teenagers pride in the fact that America's leading poet was gay was rejected by all the local media around Camden and Philadelphia. The Walt Whitman Poetry Center refused to intercede, for fear that heterosexual teenagers would not want to attend the center if they knew the man it was named after was gay. (Erkkila, 153–154) The issue is not so much what the truth was. The issue is whether America wants to know that truth. So the image of Walt Whitman has been commodified, or scrubbed clean, in order to give America a national bard it can live with, and as we have seen, Whitman himself was the leader of such efforts.

There are two museums dedicated to the "Good Gray Poet," one in his first home and one in his last. His birthplace in Huntington, Long Island is a reconstructed house complete with typical furnishings of the period, but the things that actually belonged to the Whitman family have been lost in the nearly two centuries since he lived there as a child of three. The house on Mickle Boulevard in Camden is the best place to get a sense of Whitman the man. There one may find the chairs he sat in, the round felt hat he wore, and the bed he died in. From that museum it is only a short ride to his tomb in Harleigh Cemetery, where he is buried above ground with half a dozen members of his family. Its stone entryway is plain, but it cost more than his house and seems a bit grander than one might expect of a simple man of the people.

The physical images that remain behind are a collection of some 137 photographs and several paintings. Eager to concretize his memory—even while he purposely obscured some elements of his life—Whitman was the most painted and photographed poet of his century. He had himself photographed with expressions laughing and serious, alone and with his caretakers, playing with children and staring gladly into Peter Doyle's eyes. Perhaps the most revealing photograph is one in which his arm is raised, with a butterfly perched on his extended finger as if to indicate his intimacy with the natural world. Long after it was taken, people realized that he was wearing a sweater in it, a sure sign that it was not butterfly weather. Of course, it was a posed photograph taken in a studio with a paper butterfly, attached to his finger by a bit of wire, a perfect example of Walt Whitman's showmanship. The butterfly was later found in a trunk. Even more "revealing" is a recently unearthed set of seven nude photographic studies taken by the painter Thomas Eakins, who recorded many of his subjects in this manner. These pictures show us an old man of nearly seventy, unashamed of his body, graceful and masculine still.

The real Whitman was captured in another way when Thomas Edison had his voice recorded reading his poem "America" on a cylinder in 1890. The cylinder was filed away for decades and did not reappear until it was discovered in a Texas library in the 1950s, when it was transferred to audiotape and forgotten again for several decades. Scholars have had it augmented in order to authenticate it. As one might expect, it is a rich baritone voice, but what proved it real was the flat New Jersey accent, consistent with a speaker of Whitman's time and place. It is commonplace to hear recorded voices of the poets of the 20th century, but it is almost ghostly to hear this voice from another era proudly declaiming patriotic verses.

Whitman's words, of course, are his most tangible bequest. Along with the poems of *Leaves of Grass*, his essays, stories, editorials, diaries and letters remain. Excerpted phrases from his work have become the titles of modern books, such as E.M. Forster's *A Passage to India*, F. Scott Fitzgerald's *Tender is the Night*, and Ray Bradbury's *I Sing the Body Electric*. Films entitled with his words include *Now, Voyager* and *Goodbye My Fancy*, and plays include Sutton Vane's *Outward Bound* and Larry Kramer's *The Destiny of Me*. Many composers, such as Charles Ives and Ned Rorem, have set his poems to music.

Perhaps Whitman's most important legacy, however, is his vision. The three main strands of his thought—democracy, spirituality, and homoeroticism—are woven together in an eloquent footnote to "Democratic Vistas," when he foresees a future for America in which loving comradeship becomes the spiritual counterbalance for vulgar materialism:

> Many will say it is a dream and will not follow my inferences; but I confidently expect a time when there will be seen, running like a half-hid warp through all the myriad audible and visible worldly interests of America, threads of manly friendship, fond and loving, pure and sweet, strong and life-long, carried to degrees hitherto unknown—not only giving tone to individual character, and making it unprecedently emotional, muscular, heroic, and refined, but having the deepest relations to general politics. I say democracy infers such loving comradeship, as its most inevitable

twin or counterpart, without which it will be incomplete, in vain, and incapable of perpetuating itself.

For the first two-thirds of the 20th century, the paradigm for gay men was the witty urbane sophisticate, somewhat foppish and slightly effeminate, embodied by Oscar Wilde. From the 1960s onward, it was Walt Whitman who was the model: earthy, natural, sincere and—at least in outward appearance and manner—masculine. It took more than a century for his "descendants" to catch up to him.

Walt Whitman lived at a crucial moment in gay history. "Prior to Whitman there were homosexual acts but no homosexuals. Whitman coincides with and defines a radical change in historical consciousness: the self-conscious awareness of homosexuality as identity." (Martin, 51–2) It was his voice, sometimes clarion, sometimes faltering, that first began to summon a new community of loving comrades into existence, a dream that would not be fully realized until the century after his. That he managed to become his nation's most revered poet in spite of—or because of—his homosexual sensibility is a testament to the universality of same-sex love.

At their best, Whitman's words were unforgettably graceful and strong. Only in our own time has their true import been revealed, as newly liberated gay readers explain to the world the special significance these words hold for them. Even though Whitman felt he had to deny himself, his promise to the gay readers who were to come after him has been fulfilled:

O you shunn'd persons, I at least do not shun you,
I come forthwith in your midst, I will be your poet,
I will be more to you than to any of the rest.

Allen, Gay Wilson. *The Solitary Singer.* New York: Grove Press, 1955.

Arthur, Gavin. *The Circle of Sex.* San Francisco: Panagraphic Press, 1962.

Arvin, Newton. *Whitman.* New York: The Macmillan Company, 1938.

Asselineau, Roger. *The Evolution of Walt Whitman.* Iowa City: University of Iowa Press, 1999.

Bergman, David. *Gaiety Transfigured: Gay Self-Representation in American Literature.* Madison: The University of Wisconsin Press, 1991.

Bertz, Edward. "Walt Whitman, ein Charakterbild" in *Jahrbuch fur sexuelle Zwischenstufen,* 1905.

Bucke, Richard Maurice. *Cosmic Consciousness.* New York: Citadel Press, 1970.

Canby, Henry Seidel. *Walt Whitman: An American.* Boston: Houghton Mifflin Company, 1943.

Carpenter, Edward. *Days with Walt Whitman.* New York: The Macmillan Company, 1908.

Cavitch, David. *My Soul and I: The Inner Life of Walt Whitman.* Boston: Beacon Press, 1985.

Coghill, Sheila and Thom Tammaro. *Visiting Walt: Poems Inspired by the Life and Work of Walt Whitman.* Iowa City: University of Iowa Press, 2003.

Cowley, Malcolm. "Introduction," in *Walt Whitman's Leaves of Grass: His Original Edition.* New York: Viking Press, 1959.

Duberman, Martin Bauml. "1913 Walt Whitman's Anomaly," in *About Time: Exploring the Gay Past.* New York: Gay Presses of New York, 1986.

Erkkila, Betsy. "Whitman and the Homosexual Republic," in *Walt Whitman: The Centennial Essays,* ed. Ed Folsom. Iowa City: University of Iowa Press, 1994.

Fiedler, Leslie A. "Images of Walt Whitman," in *Leaves of Grass: One Hundred Years After,* ed. Milton Hindus. Stanford: Stanford University Press, 1955. 55–73.

Fone, Byrne R.S. *Masculine Landscapes: Walt Whitman and the Homo-erotic Text.* Carbondale: Southern Illinois University Press, 1992.

Holloway, Emory. "Walt Whitman's Love Affairs." *Dial,* November 1920. 473–83.

———. *Whitman: An Interpretation in Narrative.* New York: Alfred Knopf, 1926.

Kaplan, Justin. *Walt Whitman: A Life.* New York: Simon and Schuster, 1980.

———. "The Biographer's Problem," in *Walt Whitman of Mickle Street: A Centennial Collection.* ed. Geoffrey M. Still. Knoxville: University of Tennessee Press, 1994.

Lawrence, David Herbert. "Whitman," in *Studies in Classic American Literature.* New York: Penguin Books, 1977.

Loving, Jerome. *Walt Whitman: The Song of Himself.* Berkeley: University of California Press, 1999.

Martin, Robert K. *The Homosexual Tradition in American Poetry.* Austin: University of Texas Press, 1979.

Matthiessen, F.O. *American Renaissance: Art and Expression in the Age of Emerson and Whitman.* New York: Oxford University Press, 1941.

Myerson, Joel, ed. *Whitman in his Own Time: A Biographical Chronicle of His Life, Drawn from Recollections, Memoirs, and Interviews by Friends and Associates.* Iowa City: University of Iowa Press, 1991.

Perlman, Jim, Ed Folsom, and Dan Campion, ed. *Walt Whitman: The Measure of His Song.* 2nd edition. Duluth, MN: Holy Cow! Press, 1998.

Perry, Bliss. *American Men of Letters: Walt Whitman.* Boston: Houghton Mifflin Company, 1906.

Reynolds, David S. *Walt Whitman: A Cultural Biography.* New York: Alfred A. Knopf, 1995.

Rivers, W.C. *Walt Whitman's Anomaly.* London: 1913.

Saunders, Henry S., ed. *Parodies on Walt Whitman.* New York: American Library Service, 1923.

Schmidgall, Gary. *Walt Whitman: A Gay Life.* New York: Dutton, 1997.

Sedgwick, Eve Kosofsky. "Toward the Twentieth Century: English Readers of Whitman" in *Between Men: English Literature and Male Homosexual Desire.* New York: Columbia University Press, 1985.

Shively, Charley. *Calamus Lovers: Walt Whitman's Working Class Camerados.* San Francisco: Gay Sunshine Press, 1987.

Symonds, John Addington. "A Problem in Modern Ethics," in *Male Love*, ed. John Lauritsen. New York: Pagan Press, 1983.

Traubel, Horace. *With Walt Whitman in Camden* (9 volumes). Vol. 1. New York: Rowman and Littlefield, Inc. 1961.

Van Doren, Mark. "Walt Whitman, Stranger," in *American Mercury.* July 1935.

Warner, Michael. "Introduction." *The Portable Walt Whitman.* New York: Penguin Group, 2004.

Werth, Barry. *The Scarlet Professor—Newton Arvin: A Literary Life Shattered by Scandal.* New York: Random House, Inc., 2001.

Zweig, Paul. *Walt Whitman: The Making of the Poet.* New York: Basic Books, Inc., 1984.

1819	Born May 31 at West Hills, near Huntington, Long Island, New York.
1823	Family moves to Brooklyn, New York.
1825–30	Attends public school in Brooklyn.
1830–35	Works at printing trade in New York City.
1836–41	Teaches on Long Island.
1842–49	Edits newspapers: *Aurora, Evening Tatler, Brooklyn Daily Eagle, Brooklyn Freeman*, etc.
1848	Travels to New Orleans; edits *The Crescent*.
1850–54	Runs printing office and stationery store in New York.
1855	1st edition *Leaves of Grass* printed. Father dies.
1856	2nd edition *Leaves of Grass* printed. Thoreau and Alcott visit.
1857–59	Edits *Brooklyn Times*. Meets Fred Vaughan. Frequents Pfaff's Tavern.
1860	3rd edition *Leaves of Grass* printed, including homoerotic "Calamus" poems. Visits Emerson in Boston and refuses to censor erotic "Children of Adam" poems. Meets William Douglas O'Connor.
1862	Goes to Fredericksburg, Virginia to find brother George, wounded in Civil War.
1863–65	Visits wounded soldiers in Washington, D.C. Infatuated with Lewis K. Brown and Thomas P. Sawyer.
1865	Works as clerk in Bureau of Indian Affairs. Lincoln assassinated. *Drum Taps and Sequel* printed with "When Lilacs Last in the Dooryard Bloom'd." Fired from Bureau of Indian Affairs and goes to work for Attorney General. Meets Peter Doyle.
1866	William Douglas O'Connor publishes *The Good Gray Poet*.
1867	4th edition *Leaves of Grass* published.

1868	Poems of Walt Whitman (expurgated) published in England.
1870	Anguished diary entry about Peter Doyle.
1871	5th edition *Leaves of Grass* published. "Democratic Vistas" and "Passage to India" published.
1873	Suffers paralytic stroke. Mother dies. Moves to Camden, New Jersey.
1874	"Song of the Redwood Tree" and "Prayer of Columbus" published.
1876	6th ("Centennial") edition *Leaves of Grass* and *Two Rivulets* published. Meets Harry Stafford. Recuperates at White Horse Farm. Anne Gilchrist moves to Philadelphia to court Whitman.
1877	Edward Carpenter visits. Dr. R.M. Bucke visits.
1879	Gives first Lincoln lecture. Anne Gilchrist returns to England. Travels to Kansas and Colorado. Visits brother Jeff in St. Louis for three months.
1880	Visits Dr. Bucke in Ontario, Canada.
1881	7th edition *Leaves of Grass* published.
1882	Oscar Wilde visits.
1884	Buys house at 328 (later 330) Mickle Street, Camden. Bram Stoker visits.
1885	Suffers sunstroke. Given horse and carriage. Anne Gilchrist dies.
1888	8th edition Leaves of Grass published, along with *Specimen Days & Collect* and *November Boughs* under title *Complete Poems & Prose of Walt Whitman.* Horace Traubel begins to record daily conversations. Suffers serious stroke.
1889	*Sands at Seventy* and "A Backward Glance o'er Travel'd Roads" published.
1890	Receives letter from John Addington Symonds inquiring about the sexuality in the "Calamus" poems. Writes emotional response falsely claiming six children.

1892   Dies, March 26 in Camden. 9th ("Deathbed") edition
Leaves of Grass published.

Leaves of Grass
  1855
  1856
  1860 (First appearance of "Children of Adam" and "Calamus" sections)
  1867
  1871
  1876 ("Centennial" edition, Reprint of 1871 edition)
  1881
  1888 (Reprint of 1881 edition)
  1892 ("Deathbed" edition)
Drum Taps
  1865
"Democratic Vistas"
  1867
Two Rivulets
  1876
Complete Poems and Prose (Includes *Specimen Days* and *November Boughs*)
  1888
Sands at Seventy
"A Backward Glance O'er Travel'd Roads"
  1889

Allen, Gay Wilson. *The Solitary Singer*. New York: Grove Press, 1955.

Allen, Gay Wilson and Ed Folsom, ed. *Walt Whitman and the World*. Iowa City: University of Iowa Press, 1995.

Asselineau, Roger. *The Evolution of Walt Whitman*. Iowa City: University of Iowa Press, 1999.

Bucke, Richard Maurice. *Cosmic Consciousness*. New York: Citadel Press, 1970.

Coghill, Sheila and Thom Tammaro. *Visiting Walt: Poems Inspired by the Life and Work of Walt Whitman*. Iowa City: University of Iowa Press, 2003.

Erkkila, Betsy. *Whitman: The Political Poet*. New York: Oxford University Press, 1989.

Fiedler, Leslie A. "Images of Walt Whitman," in *Leaves of Grass: One Hundred Years After,* Milton Hindus, ed. Stanford: Stanford University Press, 1955. 55–73.

Folsom, Ed, ed. *Walt Whitman Quarterly Review*. 308 English Philosophy Building, The University of Iowa, Iowa City, IA 52242.

Fone, Byrne. *Masculine Landscapes: Walt Whitman and the Homoerotic Text*. Carbondale: Southern Illinois University Press, 1992.

Kaplan, Justin. *Walt Whitman: A Life*. New York: Simon and Schuster, 1980.

Katz, Jonathan Ned. *Gay American History*. New York: Thomas Y. Crowell Co., 1976.

———. *Love Stories: Sex Between Men Before Homosexuality*. Chicago: The University of Chicago Press, 2001.

Killingsworth, M. Jimmie. *Whitman's Poetry of the Body: Sexuality. Politics and the Text*. Chapel Hill: University of North Carolina Press, 1989.

Krieg, Joann P. *A Whitman Chronology*. Iowa City: University of Iowa Press, 1998.

Lawrence, David Herbert. "Whitman," in *Studies in Classic American Literature*. New York: Penguin Books, 1977.

LeMaster, J.R. and Donald D. Kummings, ed. *Walt Whitman: An Encyclopedia.* New York: Garland Publishing, Inc., 1998.

Loving, Jerome. *Walt Whitman: The Song of Himself.* Berkeley: University of California Press, 1999.

Martin. Robert K. *The Homosexual Tradition in American Poetry.* Austin: University of Texas Press, 1979.

Moon, Michael. *Disseminating Whitman: Revision and Corporeality in Leaves of Grass.* Cambridge: Harvard University Press, 1991.

Myerson, Joel, ed. *Whitman in his Own Time: A Biographical Chronicle of His Life, Drawn from Recollections, Memoirs, and Interviews by Friends and Associates.* Iowa City: University of Iowa Press, 1991.

Perlman, Jim, Ed Folsom, and Dan Campion. *Walt Whitman: The Measure of His Song.* Minneapolis: Holy Cow! Press, 1981.

Pollak, Vivian R. *The Erotic Whitman.* Berkeley: University of California Press, 2000.

Reynolds, David S. *Walt Whitman: A Cultural Biography.* New York: Alfred A. Knopf, 1995.

Schmidgall, Gary. *Walt Whitman: A Gay Life.* New York: Dutton, 1997.

Shively, Charley. *Calamus Lovers: Walt Whitman's Working Class Camerados.* San Francisco: Gay Sunshine Press, 1987.

———. *Drum Beats: Walt Whitman's Civil War Boy Lovers.* San Francisco: Gay Sunshine Press, 1989.

Traubel, Horace. *With Walt Whitman in Camden* (9 volumes). Vol. 1. New York: Rowman and Littlefield, Inc., 1961.

Warner, Michael. "Introduction" in *The Portable Walt Whitman.* New York: Penguin Group, 2004.

Whitman, Walt. *The Collected Writings.* ed., Gay Wilson Allen and Scully Bradley. New York: New York University Press, 1965–84.

Zweig, Paul. *Walt Whitman: The Making of the Poet.* New York: Basic Books, Inc., 1984.

WEB SITES

Summary: Walt Whitman
www.gayhistory.com/rev2/factfiles/ffwhitman.htm

The Walt Whitman Archive
www.whitmanarchive.org

Walt Whitman – The Acadamy of American Poets
www.poets.org/poets/poets.cfm?45442B7C000C07070E

Walt Whitman Collection at Bartleby
www.bartleby.com/people/WhitmnW.html

Walt Whitman Home Page
memory.loc.gov/ammem/wwhtml/wwhome.html

Walt Whitman – Modern American Poetry
www.english.uiuc.edu/maps/poets/s_z/whitman/whitman.htm

Walt Whitman – Wikipedia
en.wikipedia.org/wiki/Walt_Whitman

INDEX

ARNIE KANTROWITZ is a professor and former chair of the English Department at the College of Staten Island, City University of New York, where he has taught "Walt Whitman," "Autobiographical Writing," and "Gay Male Literature," among other courses, and served as the advisor to the Lesbian, Gay, and Bisexual Association. He was vice-president of the Gay Activists Alliance (GAA/NY) in 1971 and a founding member of the Gay and Lesbian Alliance Against Defamation (GLAAD) in 1985. He is the author of *Under the Rainbow: Growing Up Gay*, an autobiography (William Morrow & Co. 1977, Pocket Books, Inc., 1978, and St. Martin's Press, 1996); his essays, poems, and stories have appeared in the following newspapers, magazines and books: *Walt Whitman-An Encyclopedia, The New York Times, The Village Voice, The Advocate, Gaysweek, Outweek, QW, Poets for Life, Personal Dispatches, Hometowns, A Member of the Family, Leather Folk, Sisters and Brothers, We are Everywhere, The Gay and Lesbian Literary Tradition*, among others. He lives in New York City with his lover, Lawrence Mass.

LESLÉA NEWMAN is the author of 50 books including the picture books *Heather Has Two Mommies* and *The Boy Who Cried Fabulous*; the short story collections *A Letter to Harvey Milk* and *Out of the Closet and Nothing to Wear*; the poetry collection *Still Life with Buddy*; the novels *In Every Laugh a Tear* and *Jailbait*; and the writing manual, *Write from the Heart*. She has received many literary awards including Poetry Fellowships from the Massachusetts Artists Fellowship Foundation and the National Endowment for the Arts, the Highlights for Children Fiction Writing Award, the James Baldwin Award for Cultural Achievement, and three Pushcart Prize Nominations. Nine of her books have been Lambda Literary Award finalists.